REFORMING

REFORMING

REFORMING
HIGHER EDUCATION
IN AN ERA OF ECOLOGICAL CRISIS
AND GROWING DIGITAL INSECURITY

REFORMING

HIGHER EDUCATION

IN AN ERA OF ECOLOGICAL CRISIS
AND GROWING DIGITAL INSECURITY

CHET BOWERS

PROCESS CENTURY PRESS

ANOKA, MINNESOTA   2016

Reforming Higher Education in an Era of Ecological Crisis and Growing Digital Insecurity

Process Century Press
RiverHouse LLC
802 River Lane
Anoka, MN 55303

Process Century Press books are published in association with the International Process Network.

Cover design: Susanna Mennicke

Toward Ecological Civilization Series, Volume XI
Jeanyne B. Slettom, Series Editor

ISBN 978-1-940447-23-0
Printed in the United States of America

Contents

Series Preface:

Toward Ecological Civilization

W E LIVE IN THE ENDING OF AN AGE. But the ending of the modern period differs from the ending of previous periods, such as the classical or the medieval. The amazing achievements of modernity make it possible, even likely, that its end will also be the end of civilization, of many species, or even of the human species. At the same time, we are living in an age of new beginnings that give promise of an ecological civilization. Its emergence is marked by a growing sense of urgency and deepening awareness that the changes must go to the roots of what has led to the current threat of catastrophe.

In June 2015, the 10th Whitehead International Conference was held in Claremont, CA. Called "Seizing an Alternative: Toward an Ecological Civilization," it claimed an organic, relational, integrated, nondual, and processive conceptuality is needed, and that Alfred North Whitehead provides this in a remarkably comprehensive and rigorous way. We proposed that he could be "the philosopher of ecological civilization." With the help of those who have come to an ecological vision in other ways, the conference explored this Whiteheadian alternative, showing how it can provide the shared vision so urgently needed.

The judgment underlying this effort is that contemporary research and scholarship is still enthralled by the 17th century view of nature articulated by Descartes and reinforced by Kant. Without freeing our minds of this objectifying and reductive understanding of the world, we are not likely to direct our actions wisely in response to the crisis to which this tradition has led us. Given the ambitious goal of replacing now dominant patterns of thought with one that would redirect us toward ecological civilization, clearly more is needed than a single conference. Fortunately, a larger platform is developing that includes the conference and looks beyond it. It is named Pando Populus (pandopopulous.com)in honor of the world's largest and oldest organism, an aspen grove.

As a continuation of the conference, and in support of the larger initiative of Pando Populus, we are publishing this series, appropriately named "Toward Ecological Civilization."

-John B. Cobb, Jr.

Acknowledgements

WRITING MAY APPEAR as a solitary activity and the author as the source of original thinking. A more accurate understanding is to recognize the author as a participant in a larger ecology of ideas that extends well into the past. In my case, if there is anything original in my writings, it is that I recognized in the pioneering scholarly work of others, such as Jacques Ellul, Walter Ong, Jack Goody, Ron Scollen, Friedrich Nietzsche, Gregory Bateson, Michel Foucault, Karl Polanyi, and Clifford Geertz, that they were providing powerful explanatory frameworks that illuminated aspects of the ecological crisis. Moreover, these were being ignored by mainstream academics who continued to perpetuate the cultural myths of individualism, a human-centered world, and perpetual progress. I learned from these pioneering scholars what they were not able to fully articulate; namely, that (i) bringing ecological intelligence to bear on the critical issues surrounding the environmental crisis requires giving close attention to the taken-for-granted traditions of thinking that carry forward misconceptions and silences from the past, and (ii) there are multiple ways that language influences both the process of cultural reproduction as well as the more difficult task of bringing about changes in consciousness.

One of the problems I have faced is that the majority of book editors I have encountered were educated to take for granted the modernizing cultural assumptions, including the naïve view of language as a sender/receiver process of communication. In effect, their taken-for-granted world was being questioned in my book manuscripts. As I always addressed educational reforms that lead to lifestyle changes that have a smaller impact on the viability of natural systems, the rejection notices often appeared within a week. The acceptance of my current critique of higher education and on what is being lost with the takeover of the digital revolution has led to working with Jeanyne Slettom, a gifted editor who possesses an understanding that the path forward in this era of climate change and growing scarcity requires a radical shift in consciousness: one that recognizes that we live in an emergent, relational, and co-dependent world of non-monetized intergenerational knowledge, skills, and patterns of mutual support. I think she could have written the book herself. Her summaries of critical relationships have helped bring greater clarity to how the misconceptions of the past continue to be perpetuated in higher education and by the digital revolution. And for this rare and supportive experience I am eternally grateful.

Chet Bowers

❧ 1 ❧

The Politics of Language

THE CURRENT DEBATE ABOUT THE REFORM of higher education ignores the two dominant global changes occurring today—the ecological crisis and the digital revolution. Understanding why this is requires focusing on the politics of language. Without language there would be no politics as we now know it and no culture beyond what can be communicated through bodily gestures and uses of space. But politics are a constant of everyday life as we debate how to address social justice issues, whether there is climate change or only a conspiracy of liberals to promote government funding of their pet projects, and whether higher education should prepare students to contribute to America's competitiveness in a global economy that is being reshaped by the digital revolution.

Language is also essential to learning to think and communicate with others, to passing on the cultural traditions that are tacitly learned and thus often not recognized as traditions, to clarifying interpersonal misunderstandings, and to negotiating new relationships. Indeed, the importance of language cannot be understood without understanding culture, and culture cannot be understood as separate from language. Yet there are hidden depths and complexities to languaging processes

I

that are not understood—even by people who possess a talent for, and variety of skills, in using language.

The title of this book, which suggests a connection between the indifference of many academics, the mythical thinking that underlies much of what students learn from their courses, and the slippery slope of techno-fascism we are being led down, is intended to make explicit how language limits conscious awareness in ways that go largely unnoticed. There are many other hidden influences that need to be made explicit, as one of the main arguments of this book is that higher education, and by extension public schools, has promoted a view of language that supports how schools want to be perceived by the public and by colleagues and students; namely, that their thinking and research are based on objective knowledge and that their theories and explanations are the result of a rational process that is free of cultural influences. As I will explain, language (that is, semiotic systems) is essential to both the natural and cultural ecologies within which we live. When understood as bio- and eco-semiotic systems, language encompasses far more than the spoken and printed word. By referring to cultures as ecologies of language and therefore communication, I am highlighting what is widely ignored at all levels of society, and especially in public school and university classrooms: that like other aspects of the cultural ecologies within which we live, language has a history. This history frames what we are aware of and how we interpret the behaviors of others. It also limits our awareness of other aspects of natural and cultural ecologies.

Returning to the connections between indifference and mythical thinking: when the deep cultural assumptions that framed today's understanding of the autonomous individual, a human-centered world, and progress are taken for granted, then there is no need to be concerned about the ecological crisis.

Individuals, according to the West's history of mythic thinking, were able to bring the wildness of the natural world under control by turning it into a natural resource. And if progress is a linear march into the future that is guaranteed by technological innovation and competitive market forces, then there is further reason to ignore the ecological crisis, as the widely held myth holds that science and technology can overcome any breakdown in natural systems.

One of the main themes explored in the following chapters is how the multiple dimensions of the cultural/linguistic roots of the ecological crisis are not being addressed due to the naïve view of language that underpins both a public school and university education. This same naïve view of language is also one of the reasons that the public has been so passive (seemingly indifferent) as their traditions are being undermined by the digital revolution. In the case of the digital revolution, the ability to move through the abstract world of the Internet and to construct one's own knowledge from the wealth of data and print-based cultural storage appears to surface thinkers as further empowerment of their individuality. Traditions such as privacy have been overtaken by surveillance technologies; personal security can be invaded at will by hackers; and face-to-face intergenerational communication increasingly appears as dull and dated when compared to the excitement and spirit of exploration afforded by the Internet. The alliance of computer scientists and multi-billion dollar corporations keep the myth of progress alive with a steady stream of new technologies.

By failing to introduce students—tomorrow's decision-makers—to how their culture's languaging processes reproduce many of the past misconceptions about human/nature relationships, universities are undermining the possibility of slowing the rate of environmental degradation that is fast moving toward a global catastrophe. This may appear excessively alarmist until one recognizes that: (i) global temperatures are melting glaciers and further reducing water-storage systems for hundreds of millions of people who are also facing droughts and rapidly depleting aquifers; (ii) the rate of change in the pH scale in the world's oceans is expected to move from the current 8.1 to 7.8 level by the end of the century, which means that the level of acidification will eliminate the coral reefs, with many species of fish already facing the prospect of extinction; (iii) extreme weather conditions and the movement into warmer climates by disease-carrying insects will also present challenges not faced before, including the migration of millions of people crossing national borders in search of food and work; and (iv) as the digital revolution continues to replace human workers with robots and algorithms, these stateless and unemployed millions will contribute to the social chaos that will follow as the old moral systems begin to break down and we enter a world of Social Darwinian wherein only the fittest survive.

While educators at all levels of public education may express concern about climate change and promote recycling, they ignore thinking about the long-term environmental trends that will be further exacerbated as the world's population moves toward the 9 billion mark. That is, while they may give lip service to being concerned about the changes occurring in the Earth's natural systems, few have given any attention to the reforms needed for the lifestyle changes that will reduce human impact on natural systems. The inability of both public school teachers and university professors (including professors in the environmental sciences) to address the cultural/linguistic roots of the ecological crisis—which is necessary for reforms to avoid the mistakes of the past—can in part be traced to the lack of understanding of the complexity of the languaging processes that people, including university graduates, take for granted.

Michel Foucault's insight about the nature of power, which is integral to the use of language, is useful for recognizing the political nature of language that extends well beyond thinking in terms of social policy debates to the framing of ideological agendas. As Foucault put it,

> what defines a relationship of power is that it is a mode of action which does not act directly or immediately on others. Instead it acts upon their actions: an action upon an action, on existing actions or on those which may arise in the present or future. (1982, 220)

Substituting the word "language" for "power" in the following statement brings out more clearly that languaging processes are far more complex than the simple act of communicating one's ideas to others and putting them into print. Rather it highlights the language/power/political relationships that exist in all cultural ecologies. Again, quoting Foucault:

> In itself the exercise of power is not violence; nor is it a consent which, implicitly, is renewable. It is a total structure of actions

brought to bear upon possible actions; it incites, it induces, it seduces, it makes easier or more difficult; in the extreme it constrains or forbids absolutely; it is nevertheless always a way of acting upon an acting subject by virtue of their acting or being capable of actions. A set of actions upon other actions. (220)

We have only to compare Foucault's description of the ecology of power with the power/politics/nexus that is an integral part of all political debates, that underlies the computer scientists' explanation of how computer intelligence will surpass human intelligence, and that is integral to how Elizabeth Kolbert's book, *The Sixth Extinction* (2014), changes the conversations and actions of some people.

When we consider the other aspects of language that are central to the exercise of power—the spoken word, the smile or look of disdain, the historically laden metaphor, the root metaphor that simultaneously illuminates and hides, and the metaphors that lead to creating life-enhancing and destroying technologies and economic systems—it then becomes obvious that understanding how language has the potential both to limit and to empower requires close attention. Different uses of language introduce changes in cultural patterns, including human consciousness and behavior.

The different languaging processes that both classroom teachers and university professors fail to bring to the attention of students, which will be considered in the following chapters, need to be situated in specific historical and cultural contexts. For example, few graduates are aware (i) that words have a history, (ii) that most words are metaphors whose meanings were framed by the choice of analogs settled upon in earlier times when there was no awareness of environmental limits or the taken-for-granted assumptions of their own culture, (iii) that the relational and emergent world in which we live is misrepresented by an uncritical reliance upon print and now data—and by the use of English nouns that misrepresent the world as fixed and made up of autonomous entities. Nor are they likely to be aware of how print promotes abstract thinking, nor what is problematic about abstract thinking, including how it leads to the reification of ideas and values. The ways in which abstract thinking undermines the exercise of ecological intelligence, and how the exercise of ecological intelligence differs from individual intelligence, are also not likely to be understood by most professors and nearly all classroom teachers. All of these language issues will be discussed in terms of how they ignore the historical roots of the ecological crisis and contribute to economic and technology policies that undermine both democracy and the achievement of a more socially just society.

The digital revolution is currently colonizing our own as well as other cultures by substituting data, increased efficiencies, and personal convenience for the cultural traditions of personal privacy, community, self-sufficiency, memory, and moral reciprocity. If university reform is to address this revolution as well as the conceptual roots of the ecological crisis, then it is necessary to consider why academics have overlooked the ecology of language. Reform needs to explain the failure of academics to recognize why the idea of progress cannot be reconciled with exploitation of the environment (and has turned vast Texas-size expanses of the world's ocean into floating garbage dumps). It is difficult to understand academics' failure to recognize that the centuries-old ideas of Western philosophers are examples of ethnocentric thinking, and that culturally uninformed ideas and theories should not be used today as the basis of a political and economic agenda being imposed on the rest of the world. Explaining the failure of most academics to consider how their courses may be complicit in reinforcing the deep cultural assumptions that provided the conceptual direction and moral legitimacy to the Industrial Revolution leads back to considering their naïve yet self-serving view of language as a conduit (sender/receiver) process of communication. This process marginalizes awareness that words have a history; that what we assume to be our own ideas actually leads to giving our voice to the ideas of earlier generations.

If there is any hope that reform will overcome what can only be called higher education's cultural lag, including its reactionary transformative cultural agenda where so-called progressive and cutting-edge thinking in the various disciplines actually reproduces many of the taken-for-granted misconceptions of the past, it will be necessary to consider how dependent the education of today's professors was upon the mentoring processes that passed forward interpretative frameworks (paradigms) that were both ethnocentric and uninformed. The different social science and humanities disciplines divided cultural and natural ecologies into special fiefdoms, unaware of their true nature as emergent, relational, and interdependent. There is also a need to consider why faculties in the social sciences, humanities, and most professional schools have overlooked the need to engage students in learning about one of the most dominant characteristics of modern life: namely, the many ways everyday life is dependent upon—indeed, shaped by—both techniques and mechanical technologies. Can the answer be so simple; namely, that this was another aspect of the professors' taken-for-granted world, and thus not recognized as problematic?

As digital technologies have massively changed the scale and patterns of consciousness, do their conveniences and irreversible uses now trump the need to engage students in examining the cultural-transformative nature of digital technologies, as well as the ideological agenda that is taken for granted in the currently benevolent techno-fascist subculture of computer science? How will social science and humanities faculties acquire the conceptual background necessary for even knowing how the history of Western technologies has been influenced by other cultural developments—including the connections between technological innovations and the myth of progress?

To not give students the vocabularies and conceptual frameworks necessary for making explicit other taken-for-granted aspects of a culture that is overshooting environmental limits—or, stated differently, to silence areas that should be part of democratic politics—will become even more critical as environmental changes further disrupt people's lives. We are already witnessing the political impact that results from people's inability to question how leading computer scientists are interpreting Darwin's theory to justify their efforts to replace humans with machines that can be programmed by efficiency experts and data scientists. Books currently urging the reform of higher education, including those that recommend a return to a liberal arts education, continue the silence shared within the social sciences, humanities, and most professional schools about how the new technologies—robots, algorithms, the cloud, nanotechnology, genetic engineering, and the neurosciences—are bringing about changes in human consciousness and the distribution of wealth and political power. In contrast, schools of architecture are following the more ecologically informed pathway of introducing students to an emergent and relational framework for understanding the connections between materials, design principles, and sustainable lifestyles.

As I've traveled around the U.S., giving invited lectures at universities, and then to universities in Europe, South Africa, Canada, Australia, and Asia, one of the problems I observed is that the faculty from a variety of disciplines, including the sciences, were often unable to escape the conceptual boundaries of their disciplines. Scientists were unable to recognize that most words are metaphors that reproduce the misconceptions and silences of earlier generations—and that their current uses are often framed by the root metaphors of mechanism and evolution that are easily interchanged with the Western idea of progress. Philosophers ignored the problem of ethnocentrism and how print media reproduce abstract thinking that misrepresent the emergent and relational world of natural and cultural ecologies. And social science and humanities faculty were equally limited by their disciplinary focus. Even the minority of faculty who were expanding the boundaries of their discipline by addressing sustainability issues were unable to take the next step, which was to introduce students to the largely non-monetized ecologically sustainable cultural practices that have been carried on since the time of the first human and are now known as the cultural commons.

The challenges of reforming higher education are multiple and made especially more difficult by the hubris that accompanies the self-assurance of faculty who consider themselves to be on the cutting edge of their disciplines. Overcoming the problems of cultural lag—that is, the limited focus of a disciplinary perspective and the tendency to frame issues in terms of the paradigm acquired in graduate school and continually reinforced by colleagues—may be too difficult. The gravitational pull of a paradigm that has enabled one to move up the professional ladder and gain recognition among colleagues may make it too difficult to recognize that eco-linguistics provides a pathway beyond the silences that now characterize every discipline. When compared to the decades it took the academic community to recognize its long standing gender and racial prejudices, bringing about ecologically informed changes in consciousness within the larger society may exceed the short time frame still open before social unrest resulting from the deepening ecological crisis — from the Jekyll to the Hyde (police state) face of the digital revolution.

The graduates of the elite and state universities who now control the levers of political power were educated to think of the printed word as encoding objective knowledge, that change leads to progress, that there is such an entity as an autonomous individual who has original ideas and uses language to communicate them to others, that they live in a human-centered world, and that the merging of science, technology, (and now digital technologies) with capitalism ensures the survival of the fittest.

Unlike the auto industry that still recalls its defective products (out of concern for lawsuits), universities are unable to recall the misconceptions learned in their classrooms. The mindset influenced by (i) reading abstract social theorists who did not understand the limitations of the printed word, (ii) the culture-transforming nature of technology, (iii) how everything that is thought and communicated to others is influenced by the deeply taken-for-granted assumptions of the culture, and (iv) that impermanence is a characteristic of both natural and cultural ecologies (except for what humans reify as universals), will take at least as long as it took feminists and African Americans to start the process of demystifying the conceptual foundations of these prejudices.

Do we have time to bring about the needed educational reforms before (i) acidification of the world's oceans changes marine ecologies in ways that limit human access to sources of protein, (ii) the rise in global temperatures melts the glaciers that billions of people depend upon for water, and (iii) the one percent global loss of topsoil per year and the corporate agenda of expanding their ownership of more of the world's seeds, leads to further starvation? The timeline of 60 to 70 years we may have to slow the rate of environmental change is longer than the timeline we have before the digital automation of the workplace leads to even higher rates of unemployment and social unrest.

This timeline also has implications for the next generations of youth, whose assumptions about the world have been shaped by spending a significant percentage of their lives interacting with the abstract words and images on a computer screen, with video games, and with wearable digital devices. Will this on-screen time enable them to face the challenge of rising social unrest? As the only world they know will be that of total surveillance, are they likely to support the militaristic segments of society that have already shown an ability to use violence against those labeled as the "enemy" or the "terrorists"—two context-free metaphors that are open to multiple interpretations?

Most professors share another characteristic with a public that is increasingly willing to acknowledge its concern about climate change—which is getting easier as extreme weather destroys their homes and floods their streets. Acknowledging that natural systems are undergoing rapid changes that are disrupting everyday life is one thing. Being able to suggest the nature of cultural changes that must be undertaken in order to slow the rate of environmental degradation—or perhaps, more realistically, how to form more self-sufficient communities that are less vulnerable to the threats that the digital revolution now makes possible—is quite another matter. As mentioned earlier, the books on reforming higher education, as well as the Common Core Curriculum reforms, not only ignore the impact of climate change and the increasing dependency upon and exploitation by the new technologies, but they also ignore the changes occurring on the fringes of the dominant consumer/technology-dependent culture that is being globalized.

These grassroots changes are being led by indigenous cultures in every region of the world where there is a growing awareness that the digital revolution is alienating their youth from learning the traditional ways of living, ways that were informed by generations of giving close attention to the limits and possibilities of their bioregions. The appeal of consumerism and digital communication is a genuine threat. In addition to indigenous cultures, there are other grassroots efforts to revitalize the intergenerational traditions of mutual support that enable communities to become less dependent upon the energy grid, on industrially grown and processed food, and so forth. These efforts, which are being referred to as the localism movement, need to be part of rethinking how ecologically informed cultures decide what their youth need to learn in order to carry forward ways of thinking, values, and patterns of mutual support—including how to share and exchange the non-monetized forms of wealth created as people share their skills and provide mutual support.

The reform of higher education needs to go beyond offering courses in anthropology and other disciplines on what has previously been excluded from the curriculum because it was regarded as too low in status to deserve the university's attention, where students would encounter the cutting edge thinking of scientists, technologies, and scholars in the humanities and social sciences. Instead of exploring the potential of the old paradigms for addressing the ecological crisis, I will devote several chapters explaining why the cultural commons, as well as the modern forces of enclosure, will become increasingly important as the ecological crisis deepens and computer scientists succeed in replacing humans with "intelligent" machines that still encode the cultural biases of their creators—as has been found in the use of algorithms.

It is problematic to think that the reform of higher education can be adapted to the needs of localism movements and contribute to a wider awareness of cultural commons as sites of resistance to the modernizing mindset but still be based on the abstractions of earlier Western philosophers. Nevertheless, the last chapter will provide an overview of the efforts taking place in different regions of the world to create alternatives to Western style university such as UniVida (the university for life) and the Eco-versities Network.

❧ 2 ❧

Linguistic Roots of the Mythic Foundations

of Modernity

T HE MYTHIC FOUNDATIONS OF THE WORLD'S RELIGIONS, including the conceptual/moral foundations of indigenous worldviews, all share the common characteristic of having a human origin. They are an outgrowth of human experiences that occurred in the distant past—often so distant that it is no longer possible to recover how the original stories were transformed into narratives that became reified as the controlling conceptual frameworks used to explain the origins, purpose, and moral guidelines to be followed. In having a human origin, these myths, to borrow a current phrase, represented the "theory of everything" that guided the development of different culture—including the language systems expressed in their vocabularies, ceremonies, creative arts, built environment, and relations with their local environments. Unlike the myths underlying modernity, these myths were experienced as connecting the present and future to the origins of life. What we need to take from an understanding of the human origins of different religions and cosmologies is that they were carried forward over thousands of generations through various and multiple languaging processes of cultural reproduction.

The myths underlying modern culture, which are the major contributors to overshooting the life-sustaining capacity of natural systems, were influenced by ancient narratives we now refer to as religions. But they are different in a fundamental way from the worldviews promoted in churches, synagogues, and houses of worship. That is, the myths underlying modern culture do not reinforce a historical perspective, and the result is that the symbolic and material expressions of modernism lack a sense of history (except for the academics who make them the focus of their research). Moreover, this lack of historical perspective serves to hide how these modern myths are intergenerationally communicated. The mythic dimensions of modern consciousness take on the sense of what constitutes reality itself, which, in turn, is experienced as part of the taken-for-granted world. It is this taken-for-granted status that gives modern myths their authority in guiding the thinking about what constitutes moral relationships, as well as establishing what constitutes the "sins" against modernity. The metaphor "sin" is used here in the Greek sense of missing the mark and of a transgression against the truths of the modern myth of progress. Patriots are more likely to use the metaphors of "traitor" and "unAmerican."

While it is the academics' professional responsibility to quibble over my use of terms, the key point of this overview is the central role that language plays in the political process of cultural reproduction over the generations. Walter Ong, Jack Goody, Eric Havelock, Ron Scollon, Deborah Tannen, and many lesser known scholars have helped clarify the differences between oral and print-based thinking and communication. Unfortunately, they have not identified how the differences within varied cultural contexts have influenced the ability to recognize ecologically destructive patterns of thinking handed down from the past. As their writings on the differences between orality and literacy occurred before today's merging of print- and data-based thinking, the negative impact of the digital revolution on the prospects of a wider reliance upon ecological intelligence has also gone unnoticed. But again, the most basic characteristic of culture—that is, its ecology of languaging processes—continues to be overlooked by the current proponents of university reform, including the few environmentalists who are turning their attention to educational reform issues.

ECOLOGICALLY PROBLEMATIC MODERN MYTHS
PERPETUATED IN HIGHER EDUCATION

Keeping in mind that higher education is part of the larger cultural ecology of which there is no single cause, but rather larger interdependent networks of multiple influences, it is still possible to claim that the majority of students not only graduate with massive debt but also with the modern myths they acquired in their years of primary socialization. This is still largely taken for granted. It needs to be acknowledged that while administrators in higher education are increasingly adopting corporate values, many faculty promote criticism of the various expressions of modernity, which range from exploitation of marginalized groups, to the imbalance in the distribution of wealth — both material and symbolic — to the anti-democratic agenda of the alliance between politicians and corporations, and to the continued military/industrial complex that President Eisenhower warned about. Yet even the faculty and students who focus on social justice issues overlook the deep conceptual (mythic) patterns of thinking that must change if we are to move toward ecologically sustainable culture practices.

As this generalization is likely to appear questionable to social justice advocates (even un-American to market liberals, libertarians, and other proto-fascist leaning groups), the question needs to be asked: What are the modern myths that continue to exercise control over how most people think and that also perpetuate a cultural silence regarding alternatives to an individual, consumer-dependent lifestyle? How do these myths represent an "action upon other actions" (to quote Foucault again), such as the ability to make the myths explicit and to update our vocabulary in ways that are ecologically and culturally informed?

The basic questions that need to be asked about social policy decisions, and about who will be the winners and losers, are these: Whose vocabulary is being used? Whose earlier thought processes currently frame the meaning of words that are the basis of political debates, decision-making, and even resistance? What overarching myths, such as religion or other explanatory frameworks, set the boundaries of today's consciousness and thus awareness?

The political nature of language also needs to be understood as exerting an influence on consciousness at a level that escapes the explicit awareness of the person who thinks she/he is arguing for specific political goals, such as changes in tax policies and limiting the data collected by the National Security Agency. Ayn Rand, for example, makes the argument that each individual should pursue a life of self-interest, and that this requires supporting governmental policies that avoid transferring (in the form of taxes) the wealth of the successful to support people who are unsuccessful. What she and her followers did not (and still do not) understand is that the vocabulary, which she assumes has a common and thus universal meaning, encodes the metaphorical thinking of earlier eras. Key words in her politically charged vocabulary, which include "rational self-interest," "individual rights," "selfishness," "laissez-faire capitalism," and "freedom," are all examples of how the metaphorical thinking of earlier eras is encoded in how she uses them to communicate her Objectivist theory, now associated with libertarianism and free market capitalism. Her use of these metaphors has become the language of right-wing politicians who take for granted the idea that the purpose of government is to protect those who have been successful in pursuing a life of self-interest from those who failed—and especially from those who are deemed not to have made the effort.

What is important about the metaphorical nature of words, and the interpretative frameworks derived from a culture's dominant root metaphors, is that the dominant myths underlying modern consciousness—the ecology of words—is not given the attention it deserves in public school and universities. Examples can be found (i) in the thinking of Ayn Rand, (ii) in computer scientists predicting the coming singularity when super-intelligent computers will replace humans in the process of evolution, (iii) in educational reformers in the John Dewey tradition of progressive education, (iv) in economists in the Milton Friedman school of thought, and even (v) in religious fundamentalists who are attempting to save individuals from the sinfulness of their biological drives, and many other promoters of modern consciousness. This is a critically important shortcoming, as much of today's political discourse reflects the silences and past misconceptions that still frame what many people take to be the meaning of words. That is, much of today's political debate about education, health care, taxes, growing the economy, global competition, and transitioning to the unrestrained freedom of a digital future that empowers everyone to operate largely outside of control of government (but still under the watchful eye of the National Security Agency) is based on myths that originated in the thinking of earlier centuries.

Individualism is one of the major misconceptions still being perpetuated in higher education, and it is being further reinforced as more students pursue the online route to their college degrees.

Like much of the vocabulary inherited from the past, individualism is a metaphor, and the meaning of metaphors is settled by use of an *analog*. An analog refers to the cognitive/linguistic process of transferring information or meaning from one word or phrase (the analog or source) to another word or phrase (the target), thus encoding the meaning of the source word within the targeted word. The question of how to understand the meaning of individualism was to think of it as being like a "subject," and the analog that framed the meaning of "subject" came from the socially stratified Medieval world. The *analog* introduces a comparative "as like" and "similar to" way of thinking that involves a transfer of meaning from something already familiar to a new word, or, as with "individualism," to provide the basis for a new meaning; in this case, the shift from being a subject under the control of a higher authority, such as one's lord or king, to being autonomous and free. This process of transferring meaning—and thus changing the meaning of words over time—can be seen in the different ways "individualism," has been understood.

The idea of being a separate, even autonomous individual who is self-creating in terms of ideas and values goes well back in Western history. The responsibility to make moral choices, to worship God, to think rationally rather than to yield to the influence of the senses, to own property, to transition from being a subject to being a citizen, to engage in competitive markets, to be free of traditions, to think critically, to create objective knowledge, and now to become a citizen of cyberspace—all of these are analogs that have served to frame how the word "individual" was understood at different periods in the West. Today, different social groups still rely upon one or a combination of these earlier analogs for framing the meaning of what is taken to be unique about the individual.

For market libertarians following the thinking of Ayn Rand and other theorists who frame the meaning of individualism in terms of competitive and economic achievers, the actions of government on the actions of the poor (to restate Foucault's understanding of the exercise of power) is profoundly different from that supported by the social justice liberals influenced by the Social Gospel, the writings of Mahatma Gandhi, Martin Luther Jr., Cesar Chavez, and the Four Freedoms promoted by Franklin Delano Roosevelt. Environmental writers who understand that individuals are utterly dependent upon the natural environment, such as Gary Snyder, Wendell Berry, and Vandana Shiva, frame the political discourse in terms of an entirely different set of priorities. The ecologically oriented individual's actions upon the natural world focus on reducing the use of technologies poisonous to the environment, curbing the hegemony of the industrial/consumer- oriented culture, while supporting various localism movements—or what I term the cultural commons. Much of today's politics are, in effect, influenced by the analogs settled upon during earlier eras when there was little or no awareness of environmental limits. The tragedy of mindless environmental degradation can in part be traced to how public schools and universities perpetuate the myth of the autonomous individual who has certain proclivities, but is still exempt from being held responsible for the decline in democratic decision-making and in the viability of natural systems.

The failure to promote what I term ecological intelligence, and what others refer to as systems thinking, leads to the continued survival of the myth of individualism. This should be obvious to anyone even slightly aware of how thought, values, and communication are dependent upon the metaphorical language carried forward through different avenues of communication and modes of cultural storage. Our absolute dependence upon the diverse ecologies of language—that is, the ecologies of metaphorical thinking that can be traced back through many centuries, should have led to questioning the supporting myths that enable the myth of the autonomous individual to survive as today's taken-for-granted reality. These supporting myths include the misconceptions of both John Locke and René Descartes, namely, that knowledge of traditions impedes the individual's ability to constitute ideas and to think rationally—a misconception that is further strengthened by the increased reliance on data-based representations and storage.

OBJECTIVE KNOWLEDGE AND THE
CONDUIT VIEW OF LANGUAGE:

There is another dimension to the politics that follows from ignoring the metaphorical nature of language and that contributes to how past forms of intelligence are encoded in today's taken-for-granted metaphors. For example, to maintain the myth of a culture-free rational process as well as the myth of objective knowledge, two assumptions are essential: (i) that words are not metaphorical, but instead stand for and refer to real things, and that (ii) the individual, in being both free and rational, decides which words best communicate her/his "own" ideas. These minor myths, which have huge political implications, cut off questioning by people who lack the elaborate language codes necessary for challenging whether what is being represented as objective knowledge is actually so, or is an interpretation based on shared assumptions that ignore the metaphorical nature of language. In addition, the myth of objective knowledge also requires assuming that communication is like a sender/receiver process. Michael Reddy referred to this widely held misconception as the conduit view of language, in which ideas, data, and information can be sent to others. (1987). The conduit view of communication, such as in print, the use of data, and in monologues, hides that words are metaphors that carry forward the analogs settled upon in the past. For example, until recently the analogs that framed the meaning of "woman" and "environment" were in part derived from the patriarchal and anthropocentrist myths found in Genesis.

The need to recognize that most words are metaphors, and that they have a history, seems especially difficult for many people to grasp. Perhaps there is an unconscious fear that this will undermine the conceptual foundations of their taken-for-granted world. Understanding that words have a specific cultural history leads to resistance and to reframing the meaning of key parts of the vocabulary. While I think this is a first and essential step in bringing about a change in consciousness, it is also necessary to recognize the hundreds of years it took for these meanings to gain acceptance, and to recognize that the analogs that framed these metaphors privileged some at the expense of others. The critical question is: Do we have enough time, before the ecological crisis overpowers all other concerns, to reframe the meaning of such metaphors as progress, individualism, intelligence, tradition, and so forth?

ORIGINAL THINKING AND OBJECTIVE KNOWLEDGE

In addition to how words such as "data," "work," "wealth," "intelligence," and "needs," take on different meanings as new analogs are introduced and gain wide acceptance, there is another layer of metaphorical thinking that plays an even more influential role in shaping what people are able to think about, and thus in guiding political discourse in ways that marginalize important issues. Within the West, the dominant root metaphors, which provide the overarching interpretive and moral frameworks that influence many aspects of the culture, include the following: patriarchy, anthropocentrism, mechanism, individualism, progress, economism, evolution, and now ecology. Each of these root metaphors can be traced back to mythopoetic narratives and to powerful evocative experiences such as the successes that accompanied combining the scientific gaze with a mechanistic model for understanding life processes.

The ways in which the root metaphors of the culture frame and thus limit the nature of political discourse include how each of the root metaphors has a supporting vocabulary that enables certain issues to be discussed, while excluding other vocabularies essential to recognizing and naming alternative realities. For example, the vocabulary that supports the root metaphor of patriarchy excluded considering women as intellectual equals with men, and of being artists, scientists, and skilled crafts-persons. The vocabulary that supports the root metaphor of mechanism excludes understanding that life-forming and sustaining processes are ecologies. It excludes even the possibility that moral values can be traced to religious beliefs and not just to what can be quantified in terms of achieving greater efficiency and cost effectiveness.

That the metaphorical vocabularies supporting each root metaphor are an assumed interpretative framework, and that they influence issues for political debate, can be seen by identifying which vocabularies support the root metaphors listed above and which vocabularies have been excluded. The supporting vocabulary of a root metaphor system also influences how the world is to be understood, while hiding other possibilities.

Collectively, vocabularies lead to certain actions upon the actions of the Other, which needs to be understood as an exercise of power that is inherently political. It is also important to recognize that the vocabularies of different root metaphors, such as individualism, progress, and anthropocentism are mutually supportive. The result is that the use of words and phrases such as innovation, experimentation, change, critical inquiry, enlightenment, development, growth, transformation, and so forth, do not bring into question the conceptual and moral underpinning of the root metaphors of individualism, progress, and a human-centered world. In fact, they further reinforce the myth of progress.

Even the root metaphor of evolution is now being interpreted by computer scientists, such as Hans Moravec and Ray Kurzweil, to mean "survival of the fittest" (to use the phrase coined by Herbert Spencer). Thus, the Internet, which is changing consciousness and undermining traditional forms of security and knowledge, now has the same meaning as "better adapted," which is also being interpreted as progress. And the metaphor of progress, as interpreted by proponents of the digital revolution, now legitimates the loss of privacy and the empowering of individuals and groups to launch cyberattacks over vast distances that free them from being held accountable.

SUMMARY OF MYTHS UNDERLYING MODERN CONSCIOUSNESS

We face a double bind in promoting ecologically sustainable reforms in higher education—reforms that address how to live in more sustainable communities. On the one hand, continued reliance upon these root metaphors leads to repeating the mistakes and excesses of the last 600 years. On the other hand, ecologically and culturally informed root metaphors, as well as their vocabularies, are not recognized—at least in the context of Western cultures. Also the hubris associated with promoting the modernizing agenda leads to taking pride in not knowing what is not known. That is, inquiry and even a mild curiosity seem to disappear even among highly educated people who have expressed a concern about the environmental changes that lie ahead. They seem unable to make the transition from vague feelings of concern to making the effort to understand the conceptual/linguistic and moral roots of the ecological crisis. Perhaps they have been too conditioned to settle for verbal expressions of concern and too accustomed to avoiding inquiry that requires sustained effort. In today's world it is easier to escape by changing the channel. It may also be a matter of not knowing how and where to begin changing the conceptual and moral foundations of the culture.

In order to prompt a modicum of curiosity about what is problematic about the guiding root metaphors inherited from the past, I will list the contradictions that accompany each one of the them.

Patriarchy: While women in many nonWestern cultures are still relegated to inferior status and even physically oppressed, they have made important contributions in the sciences, arts, governmental leadership, sports, and in promoting social justice issues. Patriarchy is an abstract myth that ignores the complexity and achievements of women's lives. When unquestioned it leads to terrible abuses, but is unsupported when women are given equal access to education and to proving their abilities across a wide range of cultural activities.

Anthropocentrism: This is a myth rooted deeply in Western history, and the failure to recognize it as an ecologically unsustainable explanatory and moral framework is leading the world down the path to ecological and social collapse. It underlies the myth of technological and economic progress, as well as the efforts to globalize the West's system of production and consumption—which is being accelerated by the spread of the digital revolution. Changes in the chemistry of the world's interconnected ecologies, as well as the loss of habitats and species due to climate change, are evidence of major failures in the West's educational systems.

Individualism: Understanding the individual as an autonomous rather than a relational being that is highly dependent on natural systems and the cultural heritage suggests a fatal lack of wisdom that again can be traced back to the failure of the Titanic mentality that dominates both formal and informal educational processes. It should be obvious that thought and communication are dependent upon the layered metaphorical languaging systems that reproduce the misconceptions and silences from the past. But it should also be obvious that we need to recognize how technologies such as print and data are undermining the ecological forms of intelligence that many indigenous peoples have acquired from careful observation of the behaviors and patterns of interdependence within their bioregions.

Progress: That this myth still dominates the thinking of most people in the West, including cultures that have been colonized by Western thinking, values, and technologies, suggests an inability to recognize the following: (i) that the loss of species, (ii) the acidification of the world's oceans, (iii) the warming and thus melting of polar ice, contributing to rising ocean levels, (iv) the extremes in weather patterns, and (v) the increasing plight of a majority of the world's population, are not evidence of progress. Yet "progress" remains a key part of the conceptual and moral system that supports capitalism and technologies that undermine privacy and security. Privacy is being exploited by corporations that own the data, and security is being undermined by the nihilism of hackers. This myth has prevented people from working to revitalize the local cultural commons that are the basis for self-sufficient communities that have a smaller ecological footprint and that provide a modicum of protection from the excesses of the digital culture.

Mechanism: This root metaphor now influences nearly every aspect of modern life, from agriculture, health care (including brain research), education, technological innovations, business, and even the dominant modes of encoding and storing cultural knowledge. It provides the vocabulary for naming biological processes. Efficiency, cost accounting, reducing reality to what can be measured and re-engineered, as well as unlimited experimentation with life-forming processes, are the downside of this interpretative and moral framework. Its growing dominance in organizing daily life has marginalized efforts to understand more spiritual sources of self-limitation for the sake of others, and the wisdom traditions that should guide the exercise of ecological intelligence.

Evolution: This root metaphor, like the other root metaphors, provides a powerful and highly useful explanatory framework for addressing different aspects of the world in which we live. But like the other explanatory frameworks (root metaphors), it, too, is subject to being interpreted by people who are often driven by ideological agendas. That the Nazi scientists and politicians relied upon Darwin's evolutionary framework to justify the elimination of those regarded as unfit highlights an important and inescapable reality; namely, that the use of explanatory frameworks such as evolution are subject to human interpretation and thus to excesses motivated by the will to exert control over the Other. That computer scientists currently justify their innovations as being driven by the forces of natural selection, including the ways in which the digital revolution is leading to the disappearance of more tradition-centered cultures, suggests further evidence that one of the sources of extremism is in the taken-for-granted cultural assumptions encoded in root metaphors, including how they should guide social policies.

Given (i) the rate at which natural systems are in steep decline, (ii) the pressure on Earth's remaining natural systems from a world population nearing 10 billion by the end of the century, (iii) the staggering number of people going hungry, as well as (iv) the ways digital technologies are creating a connected world that empowers hackers and extremists to disrupt the lives of people and the society's infrastructure, we need to ask: Will higher education continue to be part of the problem, or can become part of the solution.?

The essential question is whether faculty and administrators are aware of their complicity in perpetuating the silences and myths that underlie the current efforts to globalize both the Western model of education, with its increasing reliance upon digital technologies, as well as the Western approach to economic development. The case will be made in the following chapter that the misconceptions inherited from the past have become so integral to the high-status knowledge promoted in higher education that its mission is likely to be redefined by economic forces and by the continuing and evolving impact of technology—which has always been embraced by higher education without a clear understanding of the cultural amplification and reduction characteristics of different technologies.

ॐ 3 ॐ

Why Universities Continue to Reproduce
Mythic Thinking Inherited from the Past

WHY DO FACULTY in most disciplines, including the sciences, continue to take for granted the misconceptions underlying the modernizing agenda? The most obvious explanation is that they were born into a language/cultural community that provided the first vocabularies for understanding the primary conceptual categories of their culture—as well as the moral guidelines governing relationships. Their public school teachers, having undergone a similar process of primary socialization, introduced them to knowledge still framed in terms of these myths about individualism, progress, and a human-centered world. Later, the acquisition of a mechanistic interpretive framework would come naturally as their interests turned to science. This process of primary socialization also included unquestioned acceptance of the minor myths and silences about the representational function of words, and the conduit view of language so essential to hiding that words are metaphors encoding the analogs settled upon by earlier generations. These patterns of thinking were essential to fitting in and also won them praise for reinforcing the deep, taken-for-granted thinking of others. The silence enforced by the root metaphor of patriarchy was also part of this early socialization—athough this is now undergoing a process of de-mystification in some classrooms and even in the media.

Moving beyond high school and into university classrooms led to a huge expansion of knowledge about the world, but this did not require a paradigm shift that would bring the modern myths into question. Whether it was a class in economics, history, philosophy, sociology, or one of the sciences, the individual was still represented as an autonomous thinker whose classroom work was to lead to an original analysis—that is, the student's "own" thinking. This quest for and reinforcement of "original" ideas still ignored that the language used to express ideas continued to reproduce many of the analogs settled upon in the distant past. The conduit view of language, which was and still is part of the ecology of languaging students are immersed in, was a necessary part of maintaining the myth of objective knowledge so essential to nearly all the disciplines, including the idea of contributing to progress (which, with few exceptions, was framed in ethnocentric terms).

The myth of **progress,** which was (and still is) part of the legacy left to us by Enlightenment philosophers, was easily merged with the theory of evolution, which contributes to yet another silence perpetuated at most levels of higher education. While students in different disciplines learned about the history of ideas and other cultural developments, little attention was given to a thoughtful discussion of the traditions that need to be intergenerationally renewed. Indeed, few students were alerted to the importance of understanding the complexity of cultural traditions, as they were participating in a world of change and rationally directed progress. Education, as the slogan now has it, is a "transforming" experience. It does not matter that the industrial/science-based/consumer culture, which is overshooting the sustaining capacity of natural systems, is the most culturally transforming force the world has ever encountered. Change, as every college graduate has learned, is the basis of progress.

Graduate students with their eye on a career in higher education moved to the next level. This is the life of the mind, where stimulating conversations with colleagues are common occurrences, where interacting with bright and open-minded students still outweighs the challenges of motivating students who simply want the degree for employment purposes, and where pushing the boundaries of understanding within the discipline is a personal challenge and source of interaction with others who share similar interests. This, of course, is the idealized image—how university presidents want to represent their institutions. But conversations with colleagues who shared similar environmental interests were never part of my experience during more than 40 years of teaching at a number of universities. The wide-ranging exchange of ideas and questions experienced as a graduate student were never repeated as a faculty member—not even during my association with faculty in the University of Oregon's Honors College and the Center for Environmental Studies. Everyone had their own horse to ride and intellectual territory to protect.

The more important question is whether graduate study with mentors who largely reproduced the paradigm of their mentors, and so on back through the generations, led to abandoning the core myths underlying a progressive, individually and anthropocentrically centered, and patriarchal worldview. For the majority of graduate students on their way to becoming a faculty member in one of the social sciences and humanities—including psychology, cognitive science, and computer science—the core myths underlying modernity continued to be reinforced. If these myths were questioned, for example, in a sociology class, and the students were exposed to Marxism as an alternative paradigm, students were still reinforced for expressing their "own" ideas in ways that left intact the other mythic ways of thinking about a human-centered world moving inexorably toward a progressive future that required colonizing other cultures to this new paradigm. In considering the staying power of the West's core myths, it has only been in the last few decades that gender bias in higher education became recognized. However, recognition still has not entirely eliminated the many forms of inequality.

The biases reproduced in the mythic thinking about individualism, progress, anthropocentrism, and the growing hegemony of Western sciences, continued the tradition of ignoring the metaphorical nature of most of their vocabularies, as well as how these root metaphors were channeling the exercise of individual intelligence along historically conditioned pathways. For instance, the root metaphor of mechanism has become so widely accepted as an explanatory framework that the field of cognitive science is more focused on what MRI scans reveal about the firing of neurons in different locations in the brain than the influence of how earlier cultural patterns of thinking framed the current meaning of words that, in turn, influence emotions, intuition, memories, self-concept, and understanding the world as a source of either fear or possibility.

The wide influence that the root metaphor of mechanism has had on the ideological/industrial/technological sector of the culture has also influenced the current shift in how the purpose of higher education is now understood. The old idea that higher education not only advances knowledge in ways that lead to a more enlightened and progressive lifestyle, but also contributes to an informed citizenry essential to a democracy, has now been replaced. Now the need is for graduates who can contribute to making America more innovative in the development and use of new technologies, and thus more economically competitive on the global scene. That these new technologies might undermine important and long-held traditions might be the focus of a faculty member's research, but the question of what is being irretrievably lost has not been considered worthy of serious or widespread consideration among students and faculty.

THE DOMINANCE OF ABSTRACT THINKING: THEN AND NOW

One of the little recognized characteristics of the dominant individually centered/industrial/consumer-dependent culture is the degree to which thinking, communication, and cultural storage are dependent upon abstract thinking. This degree of dependence is taken for granted by graduate students on their way to becoming professors. Nearly every aspect of the professor's world is heavily dependent upon the printed word—as texts from their graduate school days and as the basis of the courses they now teach. Professors are dependent on print for books written by other scholars whose work is essential to their research, for synthesizing and writing their own research, for the alchemy performed by scholars who translate the spoken word into the objective world of a printed account. Now the emphasis on data and the creation of a new type of expert, the data scientist, continues this tradition of privileging the abstract printed word over the spoken word.

What was set in motion by the earlier tradition of relying upon the printed word as the highest form of knowledge continues today. The rise of modern science in the 17th century helped to remove early doubts about the veracity of the printed word. The tradition of giving "voice" to a text and "auditing" the books reflects earlier assumptions about the integrity of the spoken word. What the scientific mind-set required was objective knowledge, that is, evidence not dependent upon personal opinion and memory, the status of the speaker, or the ideologue with the most complex speech code. The authority of print, now supplemented by visual images of graphs and polling numbers, has undermined the possibility of any mass questioning of what data fails to take account of. Data is now the basis for making life and death decisions — whether measuring changes in the world's oceans, in temperatures, the economy, and soon, now, in the number of refugees moving across national borders where they are increasingly unwelcome.

Today's political debates are largely about abstract issues such as the rate of unemployment, whether the super-rich should be taxed more equitably, the merits of the Common Core Curriculum, making health care more widely available, whether to expand or reduce the Pentagon budget, and so forth. How these issues are settled (and many are not) affects the quality of people's everyday lives. But the political debates seldom take account of the complex ecologies affecting (i) the life experiences of the poor and marginalized, and (ii) the people who fear losing their jobs to a digital program that, in the name of progress, is designed to replace them. Surface bits of information about their lives are aggregated as data, with much of the debate focused on comparing numbers: of those in poverty, of the shrinking middle class, or of ages and ethnicites of the unemployed. These abstractions are in turn judged by what the vocabularies of the *faux* conservatives exclude from thinking. These so-called conservatives are actually in the tradition of market-liberal and libertarian thinking, which has its root in abstract theories of Western philosophers.

Political discourse at the international level is also characterized by the same widespread acceptance of the explanatory power of abstract words, theories, and political maps. We have only to consider how, following the end of World War I, British and French diplomats, who were highly educated in the art of abstract thinking, established new political boundaries in the Middle East without bothering to consider whether the belief systems of the tribal cultures would enable them to exist peacefully with each other within the context of a modern and Western-leaning state.

The suggestion here is that over reliance upon abstract thinking contributes to the failure of the political process to address issues affecting people's lives, or to seek alternatives to the industrial/consumer dependent lifestyle that is leading to ecological collapse. Readers may well then ask the following questions: What is meant by abstract thinking? Why is it problematic—especially in today's world, where exceeding environmental limits is understood as a sign of progress? What is the history of privileging abstract thinking over other cultural ways of knowing and communicating—and how does it affect the storage and renewal of cultural achievements now being threatened by the digital revolution? Are the limitations of privileging abstract print-based thinking and communication being reproduced by professors who now promote computer-mediated communication and learning? And how does this limit awareness of the world's diversity of cultural commons that have a smaller ecological footprint?

While engaging in abstract thinking in our culture is seemingly as natural and inevitable as relying upon oxygen, an over reliance on abstract thinking leads to political debates often overwhelmed by the fog of other abstract and thus unresolved political debates. Readers who take for granted the many important uses of abstract thinking are likely unaware of what abstract thinking cannot represent. For them, a discussion of abstract thinking is likely to seem—well—overly abstract. It is important, therefore, to have a basic understanding of what abstract thinking, and the technologies it relies upon, are *not* able to account for. Instead of relying upon a dictionary definition, an example from experience will provide a clear understanding of (i) the limitations of abstract thinking, and (ii) how it hides key characteristics of the natural and cultural ecologies within which we are active but uninformed participants.

The way to obtain an accurate understanding of what is gained and what is lost when we rely upon abstract thinking is shown in how people struggle to overcome the oversimplifications and clichéd understandings that often accompany putting into both spoken and written words the complexity of their feelings toward others, the nature and depth of their disappointments and anger, and the expanded insights and sense of moving to a different level of awareness when in the presence of something extraordinary (e.g., in nature or in acts of courage).

What is lost when relying upon abstract thinking, representations such as data charts and diagrams, and especially abstract words such as "objective," "experience," "individualism," "progress, "data," "love," "spirituality," and so forth, can be seen in a common everyday situation wherein people are engaged in a conversation, or playing a game, and someone is asked to provide a written account of it. In reality, this is a complex ecology of multiple pathways of information exchange, involving a mix of memories, changing insights, ongoing negotiations of meaning, the use of body language to send messages that are best not spoken, changes in inner states of emotions, and questions that cannot be asked. What we obtain from the written account is an over simplification of the communication flow, reduced to multiple actions upon the actions of an Other. In most instances, the written account will have been heavily influenced by the taken-for-granted thinking of the observer who is writing it all down. It is in the process of producing a written account that the simplification and deep levels of distortion occur. It is in the written account, even by a skilled observer and writer, when the impermanent, relational, and co-dependent reality of the exchange is replaced by the appearance of a fixed event, frozen in time — this latter being the key characteristic of abstract thinking.

Oral traditions also misrepresent and simplify due to reliance upon abstract words, and especially English nouns that reinforce the idea of distinct entities rather than a relational and emergent world. Face-to-face relationships with others who share many of the same understandings may overcome the degree of simplification that accompanies written accounts and the use of metaphorical language that is poorly suited to communication. Unlike the fixed status of what is put into print, face-to-face interactions often lead to negotiating meanings, including the meanings of abstract words and interpretative frameworks. It also involves the possibility of more accountability in the use of language.

As this is less so when relying upon print, from here on the focus will be on the abstract, print-based knowledge that is so widely reinforced in public schools and in higher education. Because print has been put to so many important uses, the critique of print has not been given the attention it deserves. This must change—especially now in light of the ecological crisis and world-changing digital revolution, where data is even less able to represent the emergent, relational, and co-dependent world from which data is abstracted.

THE MANY WAYS UNIVERSITIES MISLEAD STUDENTS ABOUT THE ECOLOGY OF LANGUAGE

It is in university classrooms that students encounter the abstract theories of Plato, Aristotle, John Locke, Adam Smith, René Descartes, and Herbert Spencer, as well as the more recent abstract theorists of other disciplines, such as Milton Friedman, Ray Kurzweil, and E. O. Wilson. What is important about these theorists is that while their speculations have too often been reduced to clichés that have become the basis of social policies, their interpretations (represented in print as rational thought) are not based on more than a surface knowledge of the theorists' own culture or other cultures. Plato was a major contributor to setting the West on the pathway that elevated abstract thinking above other ways of knowing—including such ways as the oral patterns that encode a culture's knowledge and moral values. Other Western philosophers, in turn, contributed to the rise of an elite class of thinkers; that is, the professors of philosophy and social theory whose task is to interpret the philosophers' abstract and ethnically uninformed theories for the masses of vulnerable students still partly mired in the emergent, and thus nonobjective, world of oral communication and narrative.

Plato rejected these, as both emergence and nonobjective reality fail to rely upon the pure reason that would lead to understanding the eternal forms. The other major philosophers provided abstract explanations about the origins of property, the right to hold governments accountable, the need for free markets that would come under the control of the "invisible hand," the progressive nature of questioning all beliefs regardless of how this leads to (i) politicizing traditions that represent social justice achievements such as *habeas corpus,* and (ii) a view of the nature of competition that leads to the "survival of the fittest," and so forth. This legacy has led to a mix of important social justice traditions but also given universal status to abstract economic theories, such as the idea of unlimited ownership of private property, the primacy of individual rationality and critical thought over the intergenerational knowledge that sustains the local cultural commons, and the elevation of the printed word and numbers as the basis of objective knowledge.

It is important to note that this legacy of abstract theory, which has been promoted for years as the basis of a liberal education, is that it also contributed to the West's ethnocentrist colonizing of assumed backward cultures with the West's eternal truths: competitive free markets, individualism, the need to question all traditional forms of knowledge and values in order to put these cultures on a progressive pathway to development, the industrial/scientific/mechanistic approach to agriculture, medicine that excluded human consciousness, and now computer-mediated education, plus the greatest change agent of all—reliance upon data and the Internet rather than on the intergenerationally connected face-to-face communities.

The politics of representing the world by relying upon what is taken to be objective knowledge needs to be more carefully considered. The Janus god of the Romans had two faces looking in opposite directions to signal the possibility of both constructive and destructive outcomes. Likewise, objective knowledge (which is inherently abstract) puts limits on being challenged; that is, the metaphor of "objective," like the metaphor of "science," communicates that it can settle political issues while remaining free of ideological and cultural influences. Stated differently, "objective" knowledge requires challengers to possess an expanded language, including a complex knowledge of the history of the assumptions that enabled elites to establish objective knowledge as more accurate than subjective knowledge (which is itself both an abstraction and a false dichotomy). There is also the history of achievement, both genuine and ecologically problematic, claimed by elites representing themselves as relying exclusively upon objective knowledge.

Given the role of the printed word in the Bible and other religious texts, its role as the primary mode of representing and preserving the abstract theories of Western philosophers and social theorists, and its importance in the socialization and education of today's youth, it is important that the Janus nature of how print promotes abstract knowledge be more fully understood. This is especially necessary because, in their effort to clarify the problematic aspects of the print/abstract thinking connection, people tend to take for granted another characteristic of print-dominated consciousness; namely, dichotomous thinking. People who have heard only of the great contributions of print to documenting and preserving bodies of knowledge in literature, science, and history, enabling people to communicate with each other when face-to-face communication is not possible (as I have found on many occasions in university settings), jump to the conclusion that I am rejecting the use of print, abstract thought, and thus context-free vocabularies,

Aside from this being an impossibility in today's digitally connected but in reality disconnected face-to-face world, what I am suggesting is that the limitations of print and abstract language need to be more widely and deeply understood. This includes understanding what abstract thinking, including our current political discourse, continues to hide; namely, how economic and technological elites, and many of our taken-for-granted daily practices, are moving us closer to constant warfare. Resources will become scarce to the point where the state can no longer function — just as the state is now unable to provide security from hackers and cyberattacks. Just as digital technologies have now bypassed the traditional state function of protecting people from cyberattacks, the looming forms of scarcity and disrupted lives that will only grow as the ecological crisis deepens will further exceed the powers of the state. Thus, before returning to the urgent question of whether higher education can be reformed, which would lead to reforming public school education, it is necessary to engage in a more extended discussion of the downside of print technologies and now data, which has many of the characteristics of print.

What is taking an even more ecologically destructive turn is how print- and data-based learning is being further narrowed by increased reliance upon computers. Students are becoming more dependent upon abstract thinking as face-to-face and intergenerational communication are being displaced by the seemingly endless wonders of Internet and digital technologies that keep one universally connected. Unfortunately, little attention has been given to how both print and data undermine the various cultural approaches to the exercise of ecological intelligence upon which our future survival now depends. The reference to ecological intelligence, rather than to individual intelligence, with the latter being the cultural myth most people still take for granted, is important here because one of the chief characteristics of ecological intelligence is its focus on the continually emergent, relational, and co-dependent world of daily experience. Whether educational reforms can move beyond the myth of individual intelligence to recognition of the differences between cultural patterns dictated by market forces and long-term sustainability will be critical to making the shift away from the paradigm currently reinforced by abstract thinking.

Ironically, everyone, regardless of culture, adjusts their decisions in ways that take account of the emerging, relational, and interdependencies within their immediate sensory and eco-semiotically rich field of experience. This is true whether in conversations with others, in using a technology, or in preparing a meal. But the myth of individual intelligence has been so dominant that few Westerners recognize their own individually centered and limited exercise of ecological intelligence in responding the emergent and relational changes in their cultural and natural environments. Other Western myths encoded in language and technology use, such as print and data, marginalize awareness of how the dominant culture's privileging of abstract information and ideas undermines local democracy and the importance of face-to-face local knowledge in learning how to live less consumer-dependent lives.

The following characteristics of print and data have largely been ignored. Yet ignorance of these overlooked characteristics has not diminished their increasing importance in undermining ethnic and intergenerational differences in the exercise of ecological intelligence, which depends upon an explicit awareness of what is being communicated through and about our relationships. The abstract world of print and data is very different. For example, what is represented in print and as data is immediately dated and provides only a surface account of the emergent, relational, and interdependent nature of everyday life. That is, both misrepresent the contexts of people's lives, events, and ideas in ways that ignore the history of cultural influences as well as the uniqueness of self-expression and the effort to transcend the limitations of one's inherited language. Print and data are only part of the daily challenge of communicating embodied experiences, which includes feelings, moods, insights, intuitions, continual negotiation of meanings, memories, and choosing the culturally appropriate response to the evolving relationship with the Other (which may may also include members of the nonhuman world). The rest of the lived context is marginalized.

As noted, both print and data rely upon a conduit (that is, sender/receiver) view of language that hides that words (i) have a history, and (ii) are metaphors whose meanings were framed by the analogs of earlier thinkers. This means, in effect, that printed words (metaphors) make it more difficult to recognize how they carry forward the taken-for-granted patterns of thinking the reproduce the misconceptions, biases, and silences of the past. With algorithms increasingly replacing human authors, and now even being used to make decisions about who should be hired for a particular job, the cultural biases and assumptions encoded in the algorithm's program further marginalize awareness that these assumptions have a human, that is, cultural origin. Algorithms that make decisions about how drones can be used to kill suspected enemies in distant places will be programmed differently by a spokesperson representing the Pentagon than by a critic of American foreign policies. While the scientific and computer communities have succeeded in turning data into a fetish, it loses its supposed objective status when the taken-for-granted interpretive framework of the data collector and data scientist are taken into account.

The combination of the printed word and data, along with a conduit view of language, which hides that most words are metaphorical and reproduce earlier misconceptions and silences, leads to another basic misrepresentation. Both the printed word and data, especially when written as third-person accounts, are promoted in universities and media (centers dedicated to abstract thinking and supposedly objective facts), lend themselves to being reified and thus turned into universals that completely ignore differences in cultural contexts. At this point, the technologies of print and data take on a more colonizing role that hides behind the myth of objective and factual information. It would be more accurate to represent objective facts and data as a specific cultural way of knowing.

The life experiences, events, and ideas represented in print and as data, which cannot be fully and accurately represented, undergo a basic transformation (or should it be called victimization?) as a result of the writers' and data collectors' unexamined biases, ideology, and silences acquired in their own prior socialization. In effect, what is abstracted from the ecology of relationships and personal decisions, and encoded in print or as data, represents the primary level of losing control over one's life—which may lead to loss of a job, being hacked, or becoming a subject of interest to the government or a corporation seeking an exploitable opportunity. What the reader—and experts now referred to as "data scientists"—do with how the subsequent reduction of life experience to static objective information and facts is also beyond the control of the individual.

What appears in print and as data is too often used to further the political and economic agenda of individuals and groups who may not feel any moral responsibility for how they are exploiting other people's lives—such as reducing them to consumers of products they are conditioned to want. A further problem exists because of the dominant culture's heavy reliance upon the use of nouns, which, unlike verbs,

reinforces a view of the world as constituted by static and isolated entities. This, along with an over-reliance upon the abstracting nature of
print, leaves its members without a shared moral sense of order. Print,
as Walter Ong (1982, 69) has pointed out, fosters the authority of the
individuals' perspective and provides the fixed accounts necessary for
engaging in critical thought. Face-to-face communication, that is, oral
cultures, unites people as they are constantly responding to changing
relationships and interdependencies. And there is another characteristic
of oral cultures that differs from the print-dominated cultures and forms
of consciousness of the West; namely, ongoing conversations require
active participation and thus little opportunity to recover the fixed
accounts necessary for an analysis of what was said.

By way of contrast, the study of moral values within indigenous and
largely oral-based cultures reveals a lack of the subjective and even nihil-
istic approaches to moral values that we find in the West. As Alasdair
MacIntyre points out in *After Virtue,* the oral narratives of a culture are
the chief means of passing forward the moral norms that also provide
the basis of its members' self-identity. As he put it,

> The contrast with the narrative view of the self is clear. For
> the story of my life is always embedded in the story of those
> communities from which I derive my identity. I am born with a
> past; and to try to cut myself off from that past, in the individ-
> ualistic mode, is to deform my present relationships. (1981, 221)

This process of intergenerational renewal is largely participatory.
This influence on consciousness differs from the experience of *reading*
about moral values. In this latter case, the individual's taken-for-granted
interpretations take over—largely without a knowledge of contexts or
models to follow. The ethos of critical reflection that is reinforced both by
the experience of reading, as well as by the ideology that has been used to
justify the importance of literacy over orality, also promotes the idea that
the moral codes inherited from the past are, like other traditions, to be
viewed as a source of backwardness. Without models of moral behavior,
as well as knowledge of the local contexts within which moral issues
arise, the individual is free to construct her/his own moral responses.

This view, which many current educators have represented as the ideal, is itself an example of abstract thinking. The reality is the individual's moral choices will be influenced by presupposed patterns of thinking that are continually reinforced by (i) the media, (ii) the constant flow of messages in the built environment, (iii) the analogs settled upon in the past that encode the moral values of the times, such as thinking of the environment as exploitable, and (iv) the values of the corporate-driven consumer culture. In effect, the myths of modernity will kick in, thus ensuring that the moral values do not conflict with the myths of individualism, progress, and a human-centered world. This is the politics of an action upon an action, which few people recognize because they have been socialized to ignore the cultural patterns that connect.

Some youth appear more receptive to taking the ecological crisis seriously, but their focus is primarily upon restoring habitats. The silence on the part of their classroom teachers and university professors about the cultural, and especially the linguistic roots of the ecological crisis, leaves them largely unaware of the double bind of working to restore habitats while at the same time thinking in the vocabularies whose meaning were framed hundreds of years ago. Youth are also caught in another double bind that can be traced to silence on the part of classroom teachers and university professors. That is, as they become increasingly dependent upon digital technologies, especially the Internet, social media, and cell phones, by which they contribute to the irreversible technological forces that are transforming not only their own culture, but other cultures as well. This growing dependence upon digital technologies is being promoted by the high-tech industry, corporations, and industries that are increasingly dependent upon digital technologies to expand their market share—and even buy out their competitors.

Few educators are able to identify and provide opportunities to engage students in a discussion of the cultural traditions that are being lost—especially traditions that have a smaller adverse impact on natural systems and traditions, but that people will need to rely upon as more technologies are used to replace workers.

The next chapter will focus on the politics of losing essential cultural traditions and the displacement of people by digitally driven machines.

Again, we will find that the dominant myths about progress, individualism, anthropocentrism, mechanism, and evolution continue to limit people's awareness of the lifestyle choices that are being made for them by others—computer scientists and corporations whose thinking has been framed by the silences in their own education and by a market system that has no moral constraints that might limit further growth.

❧ 4 ❧

How Technological Forces and the Environmental Crisis are Leading to a More Violent Future

THE POWER OF MYTHICAL THINKING to distort awareness of what should be obvious to everyone can be seen in how the many competencies of women were denied for centuries, and how the exploitation of the natural environment is not leading to progress, but to greater scarcity and impoverishment. Instead of the mythic thinking promoted by market liberal/libertarian ideologues, computer futurist thinkers, the media, and teachers in public school and university classrooms, the reality is that we are already facing scarcities that will only intensify in the next few decades. Fisheries are being depleted along with the increased acidification of the world oceans. Water for agriculture is becoming increasingly scarce as droughts continue to spread. Aquifers are depleted, glaciers disappear, and climate change delays the arrival of monsoons and increases the severity of storms.

Just as species of fish are migrating to cooler water, people are also beginning to leave their homelands as environmental scarcities loom larger, forcing thousands to migrate to where they think they will find employment, food, and other basic necessities. The thousands of people now fleeing scarcity will soon turn into the millions, as people from Southeast Asia, Central America, and Africa will move to find the basic resources essential to sustaining life. The flood of refugees will further increase as ethnic wars spread through regions of the world already stressed by the effects of climate change.

The current moral ambivalence of northern countries to opening their borders to migrants and refugees is likely to lead to the use of militarized technologies to keep them out. Even now this is happening across the southern United States, between India and Bangladesh, and along the southern border of Bulgaria. Moral ambivalence will be overwhelmed by the millions of people escaping scarcity caused by environmental changes, and more violent approaches to keeping people out will follow. National security will again become the slogan that justifies abandoning the old moral codes that supported those in need, with the new ethos becoming "survival of the fittest."

Increased violence in the decades to come will not only be over the struggle for scarce resources. It will also come from the irreversible changes being brought about by the digital revolution. The public continues to be mesmerized by the benefits of digital technologies to (i) increase the efficiency and control of a country's infrastructure, (ii) add to the growth of the economy, (iii) enable researchers and businesses to collect and store data on nearly every undertaking, and (iv) facilitate people's need to communicate with others and entertain themselves. But the scope of the irreversible cultural changes will, within a few decades, begin to transform the public's euphoria. Eventually, people will realize what narrowly educated scientists, technologists, and corporate heads, in their pursuit of unending progress, have missed. That is, digital visions of the future do not take account of a basic aspect of human life: that people have essential needs related to work. They need to earn a living and to experience the satisfaction of developing their creativity and attaining higher skill levels. They also have a need for the social and mentoring relationships that are so essential to self-development. The capitalist system of production and consumption has already distorted these possibilities in its drive for greater efficiency, profits, and markets. But this human need persists—especially the need to earn a living.

While the digital revolution has made possible many important gains in the fields of medicine, transportation, communication, scientific research, and in basic education around the world, it has also contributed to the loss of those forms of knowledge and moral systems that will be essential to survival as the ecological crisis deepens. It has undermined the intergenerational knowledge that is passed forward though face-to-face communication and mentoring. More generally, the digital revolution has so transformed the present digitally conditioned generation that they are unable to recognize the achievements of the past. This further reinforces the modern myth of being an autonomous, self-directed thinker who is free to chose where to go in cyberspace. They believe they are on the cutting edge of progress, now driven by values derived from the root metaphor of mechanism — values such as the continual quest to innovate, to achieve greater efficiency, and to control all facets of life.

The digital revolution also carries forward the marginalization of other cultural ways of knowing, including awareness of the diversity of cultural patterns by which people live. The abstract world of print and data has become more dominant, with few recognizing how this world undermines the ecological intelligence that is so urgently needed. Individually centered awareness must be transformed into the ability to recognize the multiple information (semiotic) pathways within both cultural and natural ecologies, and to respond in ways that contribute to the self-renewing capacity of the different ecologies that sustain life.

Aside from the benefits — how the digital revolution has enabled scientists to learn about changes in natural systems and to use technologies that mitigate the human impact on natural systems — the key transformative impact of the digital revolution has been to make the world less secure from the violence that some observers now view as today's most dangerous weapon — the computer keyboard. If it were not used by ideologues and people driven to commit terrorist acts, the computer keyboard would be viewed only as an empowering technology. What is increasingly clear is that the keyboard now enables anyone, anywhere in the world, to undermine the ability of a government to provide its citizens with protection from the violence and lawlessness of earlier eras, before people gave up some freedoms in order to live within a social framework governed by laws and the power of governments to enforce them.

The media now provide constant reminders that none of us are immune from hackers or from cyberattacks on the banks, businesses, and governmental agencies that store our personal information. Cyberattacks have become such a concern that the Pentagon has announced it will release its own cyber weapons if any segment of the American infrastructure comes under such attack by a foreign country. In effect, we have re-entered an era of mutual mass destruction, such as that which accompanied the Cold War nuclear arms race.

According to Benjamin Wittes and Gabriella Blum, the international race to develop and use robots, germs, hackers, and drones is leading to the constant threat of violence. In *The Future of Violence* (2015), they challenge the myth of unending progress that now justifies the quest to innovate and to find new uses for digital technologies. They point out the double bind of developing new digital technologies: namely, that they are sources of mass empowerment that can, at the same time, be used by anyone, anywhere to make others—people, institutions, and governments—more vulnerable to attack. The ability to learn computer coding is available to anyone who wants to master the skills, which is both the source of empowerment and at the same time what opens the door to a wide range of vulnerabilities and threats. Governments have exercised some control over access to the knowledge of how to make atomic bombs; they do not control the knowledge leading to the latest digital technologies. Indeed, anyone can now obtain many of the more destructive forms of technical knowledge from the Internet. As Wittes and Blum point out, governments can no longer control how the Internet can be used to acquire miniaturized drones or technologies for turning a naturally occurring pathogen into a deployable weapon. Robots are now being developed to blend into the natural environment and used to attack a target. Nanotechnologies now useful in certain areas of medicine can be turned into offensive weapons. The rapid development of digital technologies that possess both constructive and destructive potential depend upon who wants to use them. These can range from terrorists to teenaged hackers, to the business partner who wants revenge, or to the government that wants to keep its citizens under constant surveillance. And the attacks can come from anywhere in the world, perpetuated by individuals and groups who can remain anonymous and thus beyond the control of the law.

There is also another way in which the digital revolution will increase the threat of violence in the future, and which will only add to the threats and armed struggles resulting from natural resource depletion and the millions facing starvation. This is the violence that will come as people awake from the euphoria of Apple watches, iPhones, the latest computer games, apps for everything, and the seemingly magical digital technologies that perform intricate and less invasive surgeries — only to find that the computer revolution has displaced them in the workplace.

During the medieval era, when the guild system limited people's freedom of creative expression by channeling it into a traditional trade or craft, there was little in the way of self-directed innovation. The craft and merchant guilds (i) controlled the rate of change, (ii) provided protection for their members, including care for the sick and injured, and (iii) acted as the center of social life.

The Industrial Revolution has largely, but not entirely, overturned the guild system by eliminating the lifelong commitment to developing a higher level of work-related skills with others who share similar interests. Individuals today are now largely on their own in deciding the kind of work they want to undertake and the careers they will follow. But, ironically, this age of freedom now faces an even more limiting roadblock — the elimination of work itself by digital technologies.

With the prospect of fewer opportunities in the traditional professions of law, journalism, medicine, accounting, university teaching, and so forth, people are turning their attention to developing new digital technologies. These hold out the promise of achieving vast wealth and working with others who enjoy similar intellectual challenges. Creating greater dependency upon digital technologies now appears as an attractive alternative to being unemployed. The problem is that these motives, as attractive as they are, do not necessarily lead to asking whether more diverse life experiences really need to be turned into apps, or into another digital technology that relieves people from taking personal responsibility for thinking, remembering, and carrying out traditional tasks.

The point here is not that we need to (or can) return to the medi-eval guild system (though it provided for a sense of community not found in the modern state). Rather, when so few traditions of meaning-ful work have escaped from being digitized, the sense of isolation and the need for a personal sense of purpose will lead to more innovation for the sake of innovation. The guild systems, in effect, were cultural ecologies of economic interests and skills — mutual support systems that required negotiating with other guilds (cultural ecologies). Their interdependence was the basis of their systems of moral reciprocity. The question is whether today's Wild West (individualistic) approach to technological innovation and profit will lead to similar patterns of moral reciprocity.

This becomes an important question when we consider what moti-vates the computer scientists and engineers who are advancing the artifi-cial intelligence technologies that represent the "deep learning" frontier of computer vision and speech recognition. Their ultimate goal is the development of machines that learn and perform tasks independently of human programmers. While some observers argue that the introduction of new technologies always leads to a transformation in the nature of work, it is clear that the digital revolution will have an impact different from that of Henry Ford on the carriage industry. The ultimate goal of the women and men promoting the digital revolution is elimination of the need for human workers. Period! The exception will be the small elite who have been educated to work within the parameters set by the machines, and to coordinate with those sectors of society that have not yet been taken over by more advanced digital technologies.

The development of robots that can perform an increasing number of intricate tasks, even in hospital operating rooms, as well as the algo-rithmic systems that can write publishable reports and sort through vast amounts of data — tasks previously done by actuaries — are being represented as further evidence of progress in replacing the need for human workers. Not only assembly-line workers are being displaced by robots. Driverless cars, trucks, and pilot-less passenger airplanes are now being tested. And the digitizing of middle class professions is just now beginning.

In 2014, two Oxford University researchers, Carl Benedikt Frey and Michael A. Osborne, published their findings on the possible computerization of 702 different types of jobs in the United State. After examining the routine aspects of each job that can easily be performed by a computer program, they concluded that within two or so decades 47 percent of total U. S. employment will be at risk. They also found that the mere probability of computerization would further depress wages (2013, 1, 57–72). Ray Kurzweil, one of the leading proponents of developing super computers that exceed human intelligence, argues that the replacement of humans in the workplace by computers now needs to be understood as part of evolution's process of natural selection (1999).

This is a clever argument, as it takes the automation of the workplace out of the domain of politics and reframes it as a process of natural selection that is beyond human control. It is easy to understand why corporate heads support the idea of replacing humans — given all their labor demands and human frailties — with machines that they can own and operate 24/7. However, it is more difficult to understand why computer scientists and engineers have not asked the simple question: How are people to support themselves if the opportunity to earn a living is taken over by machines owned by corporations and the already wealthy? Do the economic and social status benefits that come from making humans obsolete (and further mired in poverty and hopelessness), outweigh their moral responsibility for contributing to the well-being of others? Or are computer scientists, engineers, venture capitalists, and corporate heads today's evolutionary realists who understand that the market systems and the coming collapse of natural systems signal the need to move beyond a concern with social justice issues, altruism, and biblical injunctions to take moral responsibility for the well-being of others?

The slogan "let them eat data," which is a variation of an earlier pre-revolutionary announcement of how the poor were to live, might just lead to a similar uprising as hunger and increasing hopelessness lead to the recognition that unending technological progress is a myth that has undermined their political agency. As the unemployed become more desperate, the AK 47 Kalashnikov will replace the guillotine as the poor and desperate claim their right to exercise their 2ⁿᵈ Amendment rights guaranteed by the U.S. Constitution.

Joel Spring's dystopian novel, *A Perfect Life* (2015), provides a glimpse into the future that computer scientists and corporations are already envisioning as necessary if future conflicts are to be avoided. The Internet of Things, which will extend the connectivity of people's daily lives to key data collection centers, such as corporations, the National Security Agency, and the FBI (which has a new data sharing system with all police departments across the country), represents the techological infrastructure that is already in place and only has to be extended to everyone's electronic devices. With new gene-editing technologies (now under a brief moritorium that will be lifted as national security becomes a more widespread concern) that allow the bio-engineering of more compliant individuals, and advances in the neural sciences that allow collecting data on people's inner thoughts and emotion, the only remaining challenge will be to ensure that everybody experiences these totalitarian constraints as living the Perfect Life.

Spring's inspired account of how this is achieved uses the life story of a person raised from birth by robots and other digitally programmed technologies. These suppress any human inclinations that might challenge the culture of the "World Government's Office of Shoppingness," and its subdivision "AlwaysWatch," which ensures that all citizens are constantly being watched. In providing a vocabulary for all of the World Government agencies that provide the services needed by Perfect Life citizens, such as "GoGrow Chemical," "Happy Times," "Biostream," "Best World Eats," and "DieWell," Spring has updated George Orwell's *Animal Farm* and *1984,* which were intended to show how politicized language makes lies sound truthful and progressive. Similar to how Orwell coined new metaphors to unmask the totalitarianism of his era, Spring has introduced metaphors for the generations now flooding into the-future-is-now Apple stores. As the beneficiaries of computer-mediated education, they are willingly exchanging their personal privacy and thus security for the personal convenience, happiness, and empowerment of a technology that reduces the cultural achievements of the past to what can be digitized. Their linguistically driven escape into a future envisioned by narrowly educated computer scientists and corporate elites leads to ignoring the totalitarianism inherent in the merging of the digital revolution with corporate capitalism—which both Orwell and Spring warn us about.

WHY LEARNING ABOUT THE CULTURE-TRANSFORMING NATURE OF TECHNOLOGY IS STILL NOT PART OF A UNIVERSITY EDUCATION

Just as the myths of individualism, unending progress, and a human-centered world have been perpetuated by most university faculty, the myth that technology is both a culturally neutral tool and the latest expression of progress has similarly gone unchallenged. The larger issue here is that the elites controlling what constitutes high-status knowledge (supposedly certified by the awarding of a university degree) continue to ignore the deep, taken-for-granted conceptual foundations of their own culture. As explained earlier, the reasons for this can be traced to a number of cultural assumptions and patterns—such as ignoring that the language communities into which they were born carried forward many of the analogs settled upon in earlier eras that continue to frame the meaning of words such as progress, data, intelligence, traditions, illiteracy, and so forth.

In an effort to emulate the natural sciences, those in the social sciences and humanities made excessive claims about the status of objective knowledge, which required ignoring that all fields of knowledge are subject to hidden cultural/linguistic influences, and that interpretation is an inescapable aspect of the world in which we live. Information, which experts represent as objective knowledge and even as laws of nature, relies upon the largely taken for granted, culturally inscribed language of the person who is the interpreter. Scientists cannot escape totally from the influence of the cultural language community into which they are born, even when relying upon data-gathering technologies. Questions persist. How do the meanings of metaphors framed by analogs settled upon in the past become a taken-for-granted part of the analysis? What do the findings mean in terms of the larger life-forming and sustaining ecologies? These are, in essence, political questions, as the answers lead to changing people's lives.

Even though every aspect of the rule-bound bureaucracy of higher education relies upon techniques, and both research and what is learned in the classroom rely upon the technology of print and data, the culture-transforming nature of technologies has largely been ignored by university educators. This indifference to learning about the culture-transforming nature of the digital revolution extends to some of the most critical issues of the day: (i) its role in the production and use of toxic chemicals, and (ii) the ideology that drives efforts within the subculture of computer scientists to reduce the human need to earn a living to an atavistic hangover from the past.

Perhaps the most important oversight on the part of universities is their failure to focus attention on how the digital revolution is a creating a total surveillance system of behaviors and even thoughts. This control system will be essential to the police state that will emerge as unemployment and hunger become more widespread. Political science departments, in their attempt to be taken seriously as a science, abandoned the history of modern political theory in favor of making projections on the basis of data. One of the results is the current Orwellian use of political language such that people are unaware that so-called conservatives are actualy a mix of libertarian and market liberals. Students are left ignorant of the primary characteristics of fascism as a modernizing ideology—including how fascist countries such as Germany and Italy were highly dependent upon technology in developing their economies, weapons systems, and total surveillance of their citizens.

The silence surrounding these issues, as well as how the digital revolution is undermining the intergenerational knowledge of our own culture as well as that of other cultures, is totally amazing. If these observations seem unwarranted, you are invited to read the leading proponents of the digital revolution. Pay special attention to whether any of them—Gregory Stock, Hans Moravec, Ray Kurzweil, Eric Schmidt, Peter Diamandis, Eric Drekler—ever mentions traditions that should be intergenerationally renewed. While others may come up with different explanations, I think the reason these overturned traditions are not the focus of current political debates can in large part be explained by the taken-for-granted status of myths inherited from the so-called "great thinkers" in Western history.

The myth of progress continues, in effect, to trump the evidence of (i) greed, (ii) vulnerability to hackers, and (iii) the pursuit of self-interest that comes at the expense of other peoples' traditions of privacy. The hubris of our elite educators has become part of their DNA, leaving them unable to recognize the nature of the educational reforms needed if people are to recognize and articulate the changes necessary for slowing the rate of environmental degradation. Responding to a public opinion questionnaire by checking the box indicating awareness of climate change falls far short of being able to change one's behavior and to challenge politically the billionaires supporting the fossil fuel industry.

If technologies are culturally neutral and at the same time the expression of progress, why bother to question the conceptual foundations of progress? Most academics have taken for granted how Enlightenment philosophers categorized all traditions as sources of backwardness and superstition. While there is a significant body of literature on the cultural forces shaping the Western approach to technology, an inability to question the Enlightenment thinkers' dismissal of traditions underlies the current ignorance about the cultural non-neutrality of technology. This ignorance can be seen in the common practice of calling people who raise questions about technologies modern-day Luddites. Being labeled a Luddite is supposed to mean that the person is against technologies and thus against progress. This widely held belief shows a lack of understanding of what the Luddites were against, which was how the industrial uses of technologies undermined craft skills, reduced workers to the lowest possible level as a wage earner, and undermined the ability of workers to control the pace of work and thus the community's rhythm of daily life. Technology *per se* was not the issue—their craft as weavers required the use of looms and a variety of other technologies.

THE TECHNOLOGICAL DOUBLE-BIND

As the major writings on technology by such scholars as Lynn White Jr., Lewis Mumford, Jacques Ellul, Martin Heidegger, Max Weber, Karl Marx, Don Ihde, Bruno Latour, and others, are unknown to most university faculty, and few have asked questions about how the use of different technologies amplifies or reduces their own embodied/culturally mediated experiences, there is little likelihood that a major reform of university curricula will be undertaken. And given this continued inability to learn about the Janus nature of technology, especially the destructive effects of different technologies — including how digital technologies now undermine democratic decision-making — it is likely that the technological innovators will continue to transform culture in ways that fit their mythic thinking about the inherent connections between innovation and progress. They are, in effect, engaged in colonizing other cultures as well as their own traditions. Unfortunately, their skillful use of the myth of progress contributes to a lack of awareness of the irreversibly deep cultural changes that the digital revolution is causing. These are changes that should be subjected to a popular vote — held only after an in-depth discussion of what is being lost and what is being gained, including who the losers and winners will be.

The following questions point to how silence in the educational process adversely affects the political efficacy of people who even now give only lip-service to the importance of participatory democracy. Should people have had a voice in how much of their lives have come under surveillance? Should they be involved in decisions about the commodification and monetizing of data profiles that reveal their behaviors and values? What about the digitizing of the workplace and the loss of opportunities to earn a living? These seem to be basic political decisions that should concern everybody. Is everybody okay with how the digital revolution is undermining long-term memory and displacing face-to-face intergenerational communication? What about the ways in which our valuing of convenience and personal empowerment also empowers hackers and cyber attackers to create a state of constant fearfulness that we could at anytime become victims? Should the emphasis on the importance of data and the rise of a new class of experts called data scientists be a new source of concern? Given the rate at which natural systems are being degraded—think of oceans becoming more acidic, extreme weather patterns, loss of species and habitats, toxic chemicals altering life-forming processes, and global warming—will the obsession with digital gadgets and the Internet continue to divert people from facing the challenge of learning to live in less environmentally destructive ways? And what about the impact of Western technologies on non-Western cultures? Are we willing to accept perpetual global warfare in order to support the economic interests of the technological elites, corporations, and the military establishment?

These and other questions are central to the challenges we now face, but are universities organized in ways that would enable students to engage these issues at more than a superficial level? Are there faculty who possess the conceptual depth and breadth necessary for sustaining such discussions—and for ensuring that historical and cross-cultural influences are taken into account? To reiterate a point made earlier, the flood of books urging the reform of higher education, such as *American Higher Education in Crisis,* by Goldie Blumenstyk; *Higher Education in America,* by Derek Bok; and *Academically Adrift,* by Richard Arum and Josipa Roksa, fail to mention how technologies, especially digital, are changing our world. Instead they restate the current formulaic thinking about the need for higher education to produce more technologically sophisticated workers. They also fail to mention the ecological crisis.

ANOTHER SILENCE WITHIN HIGHER EDUCATION— AND HOW TO RECONCILE THE MYTH OF PROGRESS WITH THE DEEPENING ECOLOGICAL CRISIS

I am still an optimist about the power of an educated citizenry to challenge our culture's suicidal agendas of equating economic progress with depleting the natural systems upon which we are completely dependent. I am also waiting for citizens to recognize that spending billions to fund projects aimed at escaping to another planet, rather than being used for environmental restoration, is just part of the madness shared among certain segments of the scientific/technological community. That is, I still assume that learning about the cultural amplification and reduction characteristics of different technologies will lead to making more informed and thus better choices. Becoming aware of taken-for-granted patterns of sexism and racism has led many people to make choices more in line with social justice values. But there are no guarantees that people will explore alternatives to the cultural pathway that the digital revolution is leading the world down.

Similarly, there are no guarantees that educational reforms focusing on the cultural/linguistic/economic roots of the ecological crisis will lead enough of the world's population to rediscover and revitalize what remains of their cultural commons — and thus slow the pace of environmental degradation. The conveniences, status gains, and consumer-dependent lifestyles of modern life seem more in line with the myths of individualism, progress, and a human-engineered world than with learning socially useful skills necessary for being less dependent upon the industrial culture. Besides, if the world's natural systems are being so over exploited, shouldn't our supermarkets, store windows, and television commercials begin to show evidence of this growing impoverishment? Who is going to protest their favorite fruits being flown in from around the world, or sending fish and squid from California to China to be processed at a lower cost?

WHY HIGHER EDUCATION CONTINUES TO UNDERMINE AWARENESS OF THE CULTURAL/ LINGUISTIC ROOTS OF THE ECOLOGICAL CRISIS

As noted earlier, the proponents of reforming higher education appear to be trapped in the same mindset that ignores educators' complicity in promoting the mythic thinking that a scientifically based, technologically driven, and consumer-dependent lifestyle will go on forever. Proponents of change include (i) corporate leaders who want higher education to produce technologically literate graduates, (ii) social justice advocates who want less economically crushing access to higher education for marginalized students, and (iii) the utopian technologists who envision online courses and degrees pulling in students from around the world. Before they succeed in transforming their critiques and proposals for change into actual reforms, it is important to gain some perspective on why faculty across the disciplines and professional schools continue to ignore the cultural/linguistic roots of the deepening ecological crisis.

Identifying the forces behind what can only be called higher education's cultural lag will help clarify the complexity of the problem and explain why the deep conceptual changes that must be undertaken are not likely to occur in time to alter the technological and economic forces that continue to be driven by the myth of unending progress. A minority of faculty in the areas of history, literature, sociology, philosophy, geography, religious studies, and even in the professional schools of business and architecture, are beginning to make sustainability fashionable in the same way recent generations of academics made structuralism and post-modernism fashionable. That is, sustainability issues are becoming the new focus of these disciplines. But giving attention to sustainability too often ignores the need to reconceptualize the deep cultural assumptions that underlie the discipine. When the multiple ways in which language reproduces the misconceptions and silences of the past are ignored, then the old ideas about (i) the autonomous individual, (ii) the progressive nature of change, (iii) a consumer dependent lifestyle, and (iv) the efficacy of technology when guided by environmental concerns—these things so often remain.

Environmental scientists continue to study the changes in the behavior of natural systems and to issue warnings about what lies ahead. Unfortunately, they too often are unable to overcome the silences in their own academic backgrounds to suggest how to change the deep conceptual foundations of the individualistic/consumer/progress-oriented lifestyle, which, by now, at least, a few scientists recognize as a major contributing factor. An example: at a public talk, a scientist offered evidence of the increasing acidification of the oceans. He missed an opportunity to connect this evidence to the need for deep, cultural change when an audience member asked what could be done to avert the coming crisis. The scientist showed the limits of his specialized knowledge when he answered, "people will figure out what to do, as they always have in the past." My many conversations with scientists and careful attention to what leading scientists have written about their role as cultural change agents suggest that the problem is widespread—with few people aware of how to address it.

A key to understanding the connection between previous cultural changes, such as the ancient prejudices against women and the exploitation of child labor, points to the role of language in challenging presupposed cultural practices and values. But as I have pointed out in earlier chapters and other books, the reality-constituting role of language seems too difficult or perhaps too revolutionary to take seriously, whether this is found (i) in the use of nouns that reinforce abstract thinking by marginalizing awareness of the relational nature of contexts, (ii) in the use of print that reinforces surface and thus abstract thinking, and (iii) in the way that thinking in a language inherited from the past reproduces many of its earlier misconceptions. Academics across the disciplines, including most scientists, seem unable to connect these language issues to the ecological crisis.

Perhaps the difficulty lies in recognizing that multiple dimensions of the symbolic world are taken for granted, while the more revolutionary threat is this: that the initial stages of a linguistically framed process of inquiry—considered to be fact—will be followed by an equally presupposed cultural/linguistic process of interpretation. It may also be the fear that recognizing the inescapable process of cultural/linguistic interpretation will open the door to uncertainties that cannot be resolved short of fundamental changes in the structures of power and authority. But the academic world is not likely to go far down a pathway that leads to acknowledgment that we live in an interpreted world—and that most of the influences inherited from the past are not being recognized.

In addition to fundamental and irreversible cultural changes brought about by the digital revolution, which people equate with progress, the real change that will get their attention is when the exploitation of deep aquifers underlying the northern regions of India, the food growing regions of China, the American Midwest, and the world's other centers of food production, reach the point where they begin to fail, and the people who have not died from excessive heat face food shortages that lead to riots. Perhaps then the faculty who view their current role as protectors of the humanities and the importance of acquiring knowledge for its own sake (which is assumed to be an inherently progressive process) may wake up from the dream that changes in the environment can be left to the scientists. There is even the possibility that some faculty will begin to question the many ways they have reinforced the mythic thinking that has contributed to the country's environmentally reactionary politics.

Environmental changes that directly threaten people's lives, such as the lack of water and food, are likely to get the attention of academics in a way that (i) the cutting of the forests across the United States by immigrants flooding into the "new world," (ii) the killing off of millions of bison and the estimated 3–5 billion passenger pigeons, and (iii) the genocide of indigenous cultures with their deep knowledge of how live within the limits of their bioregions, did not. Like the threats of hackers and cyberattacks that exceed the power of governments to protect their citizens, the scale of suffering and the riots that will follow from resource depletion will also be on a scale that reaches beyond the power of governments. These environmental changes are likely to cause people to recognize the false panaceas now being proposed as the basis of reforming higher education. But by then it will be too late. Finishing the dissertation, writing the book on the connection between Ayn Rand's economic values and the Calvinist tradition of Christianity, and calculating the years until the next promotion or retirement kicks in — all this will suddenly seem totally irrelevant.

The earlier environmentally destructive energy of immigrants seeking a new life of material wealth created a spark of environmental awareness among a small minority of Americans. Unfortunately, it had little influence on the academic elites who viewed their role as custodians of a higher cultural knowledge that was predicated on the mythic thinking of Western philosophers and social theorists, and was elevated to being the mainstay of a liberal education. Largely ignored were such important books that appeared after the Second World War, such as Aldo Leopold's *A Sand County Almanac* (1949), which argued for a land ethic; Rachel Carson's *Silent Spring* (1962), which provided evidence of how in the name of progress scientists were poisoning the environment; and the Club of Rome report, *The Limits to Growth* (1972), which provided graphs showing the divergence between the upward growth of human demands on the environment and the downward trend of the viability of natural systems. These wake-up calls, as well as other environmentally focused books and the first Earth Day (1970), had little influence except on a faculty or two in different disciplines who expanded the scope of their discipline to include environmental issues — but were uncertain whether their newly focused research and courses would be recognized as making a legitimate contribution to the discipline.

Like corporations that have adopted the vocabulary of the environmental movement, academics are also beginning to adopt parts of this vocabulary. But the metaphors can easily be interpreted in two different ways. Consider "eco" and "sustainability." The meaning changes depending upon whether it is framed by the root metaphor of technology-driven progress or ecology. But as most still rely upon the old paradigm and still take for granted the modern myths of individualism, progress, and a human-centered world, academics tend to use metaphors of the environmental movement only when there is a conference or a presentation by environmental scientists.

There is a growing practice among academics of adopting the vocabulary of environmentalists to fit special events and needs, such as writing an article for an environmentally oriented journal. But I recently witnessed how this practice falls far short of thinking within an ecological paradigm. Before leaving the University of Oregon a few years ago, I sat in on a meeting of the humanities faculty that was called by the new provost. This person wanted them to discuss the relevance of their respective work to addressing what they considered the most pressing social problems. Over 90 faculty talked for an hour and half about how they understood the social relevance of their teaching and research, but not one of them mentioned the environmental crisis. Their justifications ranged from the importance of pursuing issues of personal scholarly interest to contributing to advances within their discipline. The focus was on how different faculty members, as individuals, were engaged in the process of critical inquiry. The shared assumption, which hung over the gathering like an impenetrable fog, was how their diverse scholarly efforts contribute to progress. Of this group, a smaller number do show up for talks by visiting environmental scientists, and they support the efforts of colleagues who are in the early stages of introducing environmental/cultural issues into their discipline. If those in this group were actually deep ecological thinkers, perhaps what was reported back to the provost would have been entirely different.

The meeting was a social success, as faculty from different departments exchanged friendly greetings and listened to each other's presentations. But no one mentioned the issues that should have been the focus of the meeting. That is, no one mentioned environmental/cultural issues and the mythical thinking about progress and individually centered critical thinking. No one raised questions about the power relationships that follow from claims that critical thinking is free of cultural influences, and that facts and information are "objective." These silences — enforced as they are by the taken-for-granted paradigm that is guiding the West into overshooting environmental limits — made the meeting no different from similar meetings held decades ago.

And no one mentioned how difficult it is to engage students in thinking ecologically — which is different from learning about the changes occurring in natural systems that are documented by scientists. Instead, the focus was on the current research of the faculty and not on how the forces of cultural lag within the university where failing to educate students for living in a world that will, within their lifetime, undergo radical changes for which they will be unprepared.

WILL RECOGNIZING THE CONCEPTUALLY REACTIONARY NATURE OF HIGHER EDUCATION INFLUENCE CURRENT EFFORTS AT REFORM?

The title of this sub-section raises the critical question about whether the books currently making the case that higher education is in crisis — and doing little more than miseducating the elite of American youth — will also fall short by repeating the silences that marked the gathering of the humanities faculty at the University of Oregon. Individual members of the University of Oregon faculty have established national reputations for shifting the focus of their discipline to include environmental issues, such as in the field of literary criticism. If we consider the traditions of thinking taken for granted by mentors of the last decades of the twentieth century, we find that despite increased attention in the press and other media to the ecological crisis, few mentors in the humanities and even the social sciences recognized or were aware of it.

The conceptual boundaries of the discipline meant that both mentors and their students regarded, if they considered it at all, studying environmental changes as the responsibility of the sciences. Understanding the interconnections between cultural and natural ecologies requires thinking beyond the traditional boundaries of philosophy, religious studies, economics, political science, and so forth. And as each discipline maintained its zones of silence regarding what lay beyond its boundaries, the same patterns were reproduced in the thinking of students who, in turn, became tomorrow's faculty—professors who will reproduce the deep conceptual foundations of their mentors' paradigms, with only token references to sustainability issues.

Like their mentors, today's faculty fail to introduce the multiple ways in which the languaging processes continue to frame current ways of thinking. This includes the role of nouns and the technology of print, as well as how metaphorical language (including the root metaphors derived from powerful evocative experiences and the culture's mythopoetic narratives) reproduces the analogs settled upon in the distant past and based upon a different cultural way of knowing. Other major weaknesses in the educational process include ignoring how language frames, in ways that generally go unrecognized, what people take to be reality. Inescapably, this becomes part of the political process, because communicative competence is dependent upon whose language students have been socialized to use, and a failure to understand the myth of objective knowledge gives legitmacy to current political, conceptual, and economic forces.

If we keep in mind Foucault's insight into power—of an action that does not act directly on others, but is instead an act upon the action of an Other (which may or may not be challenged, depending upon the Other's language competency) — we can see how political power is exercised. Whose view of reality prevails when the idea of objective knowledge/data cannot be challenged because the user is unaware that her/his taken-for-granted interpretative framework is influenced by the metaphorical language learned when first becoming a member of the language community? The ecology of political power becomes one-sided when it is assumed that words refer to real entities and the conduit view of language (the sender/receiver model of communication) hides that words have a history.

Few mentors guiding the graduate studies and dissertations of tomorrow's faculty were likely to have engaged their students in an in-depth study of how the technology of print fosters abstract thinking that limits the exercise of ecological intelligence to the immediate pragmatic needs of the individual, rather than focusing on what contributes to a sustainable future. Even mentors who may have introduced their students to the writings of Walter Ong or Eric Havelock were unlikely to have engaged them in thinking about how print promotes context-free thinking, as well as the ethnocentrism so fundamental to maintaining the myth of progress that has been used to justify colonizing other cultures. Nor would they question how the abstract thinking promoted by an uncritical reliance upon print-based cultural storage and thinking contributes to ignoring the cultural roots of the ecological crisis. And the question today is: how many current social science and humanities faculty possess the conceptual background necessary for exploring how abstract thinking undermines awareness of the emergent and relational world within which we all live? Are they even able to recognize that both print and data hide that this world of impermanence is also one that is interpreted by reliance upon vocabularies acquired during one's years of primary socialization, whose meanings were established by earlier generations unaware of environmental limits?

And in light of changes occuring in the Earth's natual systems that signal future socially disruptive changes, how many faculty are willing to raise the critically important question with their students that Rolf Jucker raises: Do we know what we are doing? As Jucker (2014) points out, the answers worked out during a professor's years of teaching, attending conferences, and writing, address questions that ignored all of the ideological contradictions underlying the cultural roots of the ecological crisis.

If students are to exercise ecological intelligence — which is not individually centered, and that starts with the recognition that all forms of life, including cultural practices, are emergent, relational, and co-dependen — then they must learn to recognize how print and data reinforce the myth of a world of fixed, autonomous, and causally related entities. How many professors are able to identify examples of how print hides the linguistic foundations of the interpretive process that leads to the reification of what appears in print? The question then becomes: How many students of the humanities recognize that mainstream Western philosophers and social theorists are ethnocentric thinkers, and not autonomous thinkers expressing their own rationally constructed worlds? And how many students of the University of Oregon humanities faculty, including faculties at other universities across the country, recognize the critically important insights of Friedrich Nietzsche? These insights are also core features of an ecological intelligence that is not centered on the immediate needs of the individual. As Nietzsche wrote in his notebooks between 1883 and 1888:

> First proposition. The easier mode of thought conquers the harder mode;— as dogma:... Ditto: to suppose that clarity proves anything about truth is perfect childishness.

> Second proposition: The doctrine of being, of things, of all sorts of fixed entities is a hundred times easier than the doctrine of becoming, of development. (Kaufman, 1968), 291)

To recognize the ecology of language and to see how the emergent, relational, and co-dependent nature of all forms of life undermines the widely accepted orthodoxy still promoted even in our most elite universities (that critical, rational thought is free of cultural/linguistic influences), is a paradigm shift. It will likely to lead many academics across disciplines, including the sciences, to conclude that Nietzsche and deep ecological thinkers have left the world adrift in a sea of subjective interpretations — that is, in a sea of nihilism where every interpretation is no more valid than any other interpretation. Nietzsche addressed this issue in a way that requires recognizing that every interpretation is not equally important—and, by extension, that some linguistic ecologies are life destroying.

As he put it:

> That the *value of the world* lies in our interpretation...that every *elevation of man* brings with it the overcoming of narrower interpretations; that every strengthening and increase of power opens up new perspectives and means believing in new horizons—this idea permeates my writings. The world with which we are concerned is false, i.e., is not a fact but a fable and approximation on the basis of a meager sum of observations; it is "in flux," as something in a state of becoming, as a falsehood always changing but never getting near the truth: for—there is no "truth." (330)

OTHER TRADITIONS CONTRIBUTING TO HOW UNIVERSITIES REINFORCE THE OLD PARADIGM OF ECOLOGICALLY UNSUSTAINABLE VALUES AND WAYS OF THINKING

Ecological intelligence requires the broadest form of relational rather than compartmentalized thinking. I think this is what Thich Nhat Hanh is getting at in his claim that impermanence, rather than fixed entities, more accurately characterizes the world we live in. It is what Alfred North Whitehead points to in his process philosophy, and it is at the center of Gregory Bateson's understanding of natural and cultural ecological systems. A world of fixed entities, including abstract ideas, does not require giving close attention to the constant changes characterizing the differences that lead to the multiple forms of communication circulating within and between the cultural and natural ecologies.

Knowledge of what is fixed and open to being empirically verified is thought by many to be free of cultural influences—and thus regarded as objective. However, if we consider our own responses to the impermanence of all that surrounds us, including the impermanence of our own inner feelings, moods, ideas, intentionality, and policies, we find that making claims about the objectively known and fixed world of things and ideas requires taking flight into the world of abstract thinking. This may appear at first glance to be so trivial that only academics would argue about it, but this distinction between (i) a world that is emergent, relational, and co-dependent and (ii) the supposedly fixed, objective world represented by facts, data, and now algorithms, reveals the degree to which abstraction requires living a life of self-deception. The self-deception is on the part of experts who rely on data, and it is also on the part of people whose lives have been diminished by the decisions of these experts. People being displaced by the decisions of experts display their complicity by their silent acceptance of being reduced to data, to becoming a monetized entity whose fate is determined by market forces. The logic of the market is unlike relational thinking, which must meet the test of being both historically and cross-culturally informed.

The tradition of organizing knowledge within academic disciplines undermines learning to think in the relational way required by an ecological view of cultural and natural systems. This informed, relational thinking differs from, for instance, the highly restricted ecology of language within a discipline such as philosophy or economics. These disciplines do not consider how abstract conceptual foundations misrepresent the knowledge systems of other cultures, and they do not lead to a consideration of emergent patterns within the world's diversity of cultural and natural ecologies. How the politics of abstract thinking is the politics of cultural colonization can be seen in the way English and print-based treaties were imposed on indigenous cultures across the world. Colonizers of the "New World" represent yet another example of where emergent, relational, and co-dependent cultural ecologies were ignored — with tragic results for both. The colonizers imposed their largely European, fixed mindset on the land, rather than learning from indigenous cultures' more ecologically sensitive knowledge of the behavior of natural systems. This set in motion an environmental destruction from which we still have not recovered.

The separation of the disciplines contributes to a mindset that accepts objective certainties — such as finding irrelevant whatever exists outside of the discipline. This is becoming especially important as computer scientists, for example, rely upon several disciplines of highly technical knowledge to create digital machines. These are then introduced into different cultures, with the scientists having no knowledge of what is being lost. This lack of relational thinking is one of the primary reasons that students still graduate with only a surface knowledge of the conceptual roots of the ecological crisis—if they are even aware of it. They may be concerned about the long-term implications of climate change, the acidification of the oceans, and even how the digital revolution threatens to further reduce opportunities to make a living, but they are unable to think relationally (that is, ecologically) about the cultural assumptions driving computer scientists to create robots and algorithms that reduce the need for people to earn a living—all in the name of progress. How many university graduates, having lived in communities with still viable cultural commons traditions (which have a smaller adverse ecological impact), recognize the many ways in which these traditions are being integrated into the market system? Do they understand that people will be required to become more dependent upon a money economy at the same time the computer industry is reducing people's ability to earn a living?

What is shared by both students and faculty narrowly educated within a discipline is the inability to recognize how the deep cultural assumptions being passed forward in their courses carry forward misconceptions from the past. These include a taken-for-granted attitude toward the ecologically problematic nature of different technologies—such as how the digital revolution is undermining the face-to-face intergenerational communication essential to passing forward the cultural commons. How many faculty, for example, have given careful attention to the many ways they reinforce the idea of the student as an autonomous thinker, as well as the idea that what is being learned in their classes represents the cutting edge of progress, and that the professor's rational process and research is contributing to a more rationally organized society?

In addition to how graduate studies in the last decades of the 20th and early decades of the 21st centuries reinforced the long-standing indifference to ways that cultural patterns of thinking and practices might be accelerating the degradation of natural systems, there is another tradition that has been used to justify ignoring how one's courses and research may be complicit in perpetuating (i) the cultural assumptions that gave conceptual direction and moral legitimacy to the industrial, consumer-dependent culture and (ii) the assurances that science, technology, and market forces would overcome all limitations on progress. This is the tradition of academic freedom.

Academic freedom has been essential to professors who challenge existing orthodoxies, ranging from gender and racial biases to practices of economic exploitation, as well as belief systems based on fundamental misconceptions. Without it, challenging social orthodoxies could easily lead to being dismissed from the university. Unfortunately, academic freedom has also enabled faculty to claim the right to pursue in their teaching and research what they regard as important to advancing the discipline. That is, academic freedom allows them to claim that however much their courses and research might reinforce the deep cultural patterns of thinking that ignore evironmental limits, this is irrelevant to them. To cite the most egregious examples of what academic freedom protects: E. O. Wilson, Richard Dawkins, and a number of computer scientists who are following the lead of Ray Kurzweil, are claiming that humans are essentially machines. Wilson describes the brain as a machine, a problem in engineering; Dawkins refers to humans as machines that ensure survival until the genes are passed forward; and computer scientists claim that we are on the cusp of an evolutionary transition wherein super-intelligent machines will replace biological processes — including humans. Other examples of the misuse of academic freedom include how it is used to justify promoting ethnocentric thinking, the colonization of other cultures, and the misconceptions acquired during a faculty member's years of study with mentors who failed to question the misconceptions of their own mentors.

For example, promoting the ideas of the Enlightenment in this era now dominated by digital technology is clearly an example of the misuse of academic freedom. These thinkers of the 17th and 18th century had an extremely narrow understanding of traditions. Unthinking promotion of their ideas further marginalizes awareness of ecological and community-strengthening traditions. Today, those who rely upon academic freedom to challenge the misconceptions and social injustice practices taken for granted by the wider public as well as by the larger academic community are the minority. Yet the widespread misuse of academic freedom by faculty who use it to maintain their right to promote ideas that are clearly reactionary, given the ecological tipping point we have now reached, cannot be used as justification for the elimination of this hard-won tradition.

In *The Soul of the Marionette: A Short Inquiry Into Human Freedom* (2015), John Gray examines another tradition that most university graduates learned from their professors. According to Gray, the pathway taken by the West that has led to equating humans with machines began with the Gnostic interpretation of Adam and Eve eating the forbidden fruit from the tree of knowledge. Instead of learning from the Garden's nature-based knowledge, humans separated themselves from the natural world by claiming to possess the knowledge needed to bring it under their control. Gnosticism, according to Gray, became the new religion, and its highest expression would be the acceptance of science as providing a worldview that includes the linear idea of unending progress. As Gray puts it, "Throughout much of the world, and particularly in western countries, the Gnostic faith that knowledge can give humans a freedom no other creature can possess has become the predominant religion" (9).

Science is a mode of inquiry, one worldview among many. When we forget this—when we make science the only mode of knowing or for understanding the world—it is a reductionist fallacy. This can be seen in how Johannes Kepler (1571–1630), along with others, articulated the new interpretative framework for changing the world. As Kepler put it: "My aim is to show that the celestial machine is to be likened not a divine organism but to a clockwork." It is now the taken-for-granted interpretative framework that has guided the thinking in medicine, education, agriculture, politics, cognitive science, and now computer science—including all areas of economic activity. It strengthened reliance upon the experimental process whereby empirical evidence becomes the basis of knowledge rather than folk traditions and magical explanations. It also led to valuing innovations that increased efficiency and profits—both of which gave special legitimacy to what can be measured. And like a clockwork, it helped to establish a world of fixed entities that could be understood without considering how they are changed by contexts and relationships. As a total explanatory framework, the clockwork excluded all oral traditions of knowledge, understandings of moral relationships, and that we live in cultural and natural ecologies of emergent relationships and co-dependencies.

The aspects of consciousness that do not conform to this new Gnostic epistemology, such as aesthetic awareness, empathy, memory of horrors done to others as well as social justice achievements, creative insight, a sense of the spiritual connectedness of life-sustaining processes, are either to be explained scientifically or, if that is not possible, to be dismissed as the daemons of a pre-scientific worldview. In this new mindset, scientists, engineers, and business-minded elites became the conquerors of nature and in control of how progress is to be understood.

The hubris, and what Wendell Berry refers to as scientific imperialism, is culminating in the endtime envisioned by scientific-techno-utopian thinkers who now claim we are at the tipping point—that is, the moment of singularity when super-intelligent machines displace humans in the evolutionary process. This replacement of humans by machines is now occurring in the workplace. It is happening in the fields of communication and creative arts, in service relationships, and in all levels of formal education where different cultural interpretations must be eliminated if machine testing is to achieve greater efficiencies. The idea of progress leading the world had its roots in the Gnostic's sense of mission. As Gray points out, the Gnostic promise of progress detached from moral guidelines has led to experiments on others (the eugenics movement), the Nazi use of Social Darwinism to eliminate the millions of "unfit" and "degenerate," the loss of personal and other forms of security by hackers, and now the increasing loss of the means to earn a living. The dominant challenge facing scientists and techno-utopian activists is how to reverse-engineer humans, including their patterns of consciousness (especially their memories), in order for them to play a supporting role as the Internet of Things, total surveillance, and hackers replace the human qualities distinctive of a culturally diverse world.

The question is: How many graduates of our universities are aware of the origins of ideas like of progress? How many realize that replacing humans with machines has been part of the vision promoted by our supposedly elite thinkers—and indirectly supported by professors who remained silent about the culturally mediating characteristics of different technologies? And how many of them are aware of what is being lost in online courses and degrees? Do they consider how the losses in cultural forms of knowledge will be far more important to our future survival than today's economic gains and momentary conveniences that make online learning so appealing? Are they aware of why leading corporations were the initial promoters of the Common Core Curriculum reforms? Do they know the connection between libertarian and market liberal ideologies and university research; how these ideologies continue to be the driving force behind the transformation of the traditional role of universities into the new business-oriented centers of research and indoctrination? And how many university graduates are aware of how print and data misrepresent the emergent, relational and co-dependent world in which we live—including how they undermine the exercise of sustainable forms of ecological intelligence?

The answer as to why public schools and universities have not engaged students in learning about (i) what is being culturally lost, and (ii) what is being personally lost as they become more dependent upon different technologies, may be as simple as their teachers continually reinforcing the idea that print, data, algorithms, the Internet, are all culturally neutral tools and the latest expression of progress. Again, this problem continues due to (i) the intergenerational passing forward of earlier biases held by academic elites who established what constituted high-status knowledge worthy of a university educated person, and (ii) the early understanding of technology that was either shrouded in myths about its cultural neutrality or considered too close to the exercise of human labor to be worthy of study other than how to make technologies more efficient. Now that the digital revolution is creating opportunities for people who realize that the possibility of attaining vast wealth lies in creating more technologies that will further displace humans, we will continue to move down this slippery slope until the increasing armies of unemployed begin to revolt.

∂ 5 ∂

Can a Case Be Made for a Liberal Education?

As a former professor of English at Yale University for 10 years, and now a frequent speaker on campuses across the country criticizing the "Miseducation of the American Elite" (to use the subtitle of his popular book), William Deresiewicz answers the question posed by this chapter in the affirmative. His arguments, laid out in his own chapter on the Great Books, are particularly well received across the country by liberal arts faculties currently being threatened by (i) the growing emphasis on earning a degree in order to obtain a job and a higher material standard of living, and (ii) the increasing threats from online courses and now even online degrees from elite universities.

Deresiewicz's key justifications for restoring the idea of a liberal education to the standing it enjoyed before universities embraced corporate values are significant for what they reveal about what is problematic about a liberal education in today's world. It is important to note that his justifications reflect the thinking of a highly intelligent person who still reproduces the silences and misconceptions acquired in his own liberal education. That he proposes a form of education, especially for the top tier of American youth who will supposedly become tomorrow's leaders, and who will likely reproduce the same silences and misconceptions in their personal and public policy thinking, indicates just how out of touch he is with the changes sweeping through the world today.

It is important, too, that his core justifications be represented in his own words. In his discussion of the Great Books, we find the following explanations of what constitutes the liberal arts.

> Creating a self, inventing a life, developing an independent mind: it all sounds rather daunting. How exactly is college supposed to help? By deploying the most powerful of instructional technologies: a liberal arts education, centered in the humanities, conducted in small classrooms by dedicated teachers. This is not a cheap or 'innovative' enterprise, but it is still, and will be for the imaginable future, an indispensable one. What are the liberal arts? They are those disciplines in which the pursuit of knowledge is conducted for its own sake. (2014, 149)

Further core justifications include:

> In the liberal arts, you pursue the trail of inquiry wherever it leads. Truth, not use or reward, is the only criterion. (150) The humanities — history, philosophy, religious studies, and above all, literature and the other arts — are records of the ways people come to terms with being human. They address the questions that are proper to us, not as this or that kind of specialist, this or that kind of professional, but as individuals as such — the very questions we are apt to ask when we look up from out work and think about our lives. Questions of love, death, family, morality, time, truth, God, and everything else with the wide, starred universe of human experience. (156)

> All of this explains why liberal arts graduates are so highly valued in the workforce, and why it almost doesn't matter what you study. ...A survey of 318 companies found that 93 percent cite 'critical thinking, communicating and problem-solving as more important than a candidate's major,' in part because they are filling positions with 'broader responsibilities' and 'more complex challenges' than in the past. (151)

The rest of the chapter lists the other equally high-sounding justifications that are the bedrock beliefs of most liberal arts faculty. But what are the silences and misconceptions that are to serve as lifelines for recovering the former status of a liberal education? And what are the political dangers for the larger society (including other cultures) that accompany the search for truth for its own sake, and for perpetuating the myth of self-creation and inventing one's own life based on the ideas of the West's great thinkers? How many liberal arts faculty are aware of what is problematic about the suggestion that a liberal education should lead to creating an autonomous self? What are the cultural myths that lead Deresiewicz to make such proposals and that lead the supposedly more educationally aware students and faculty in the liberal arts to take him seriously?

Are they aware that these high-sounding goals, especially the idea of "creating a self, inventing a life, developing an independent mind" are an impossibility because life begins within a number of emergent and co-dependent natural and cultural ecologies? Where in a liberal arts curriculum do students learn that the origin of the individual's supposed self-creation is largely dependent upon an inherited language and its metaphorical, encoded analogs that were settled upon earlier by the culture? The misconceptions and silences of the great thinkers that were the basis of his own liberal education are reproduced in his book. Is he, are his liberal arts followers, aware that the idea of creating a self is part of the same old paradigm now required by the industrial system of production and economic exploitation? That it is the same paradigm that reduced the environment to an exploitable resource; imposed a mechanistic, conceptual/moral interpretative framework for understanding life-forming processes; and promoted the idea of the autonomous individual who would be dependent upon a consumer lifestyle.

Deresiewicz is promoting a reactionary way of thinking when judged in relationship to what we now understand about ecological intelligence and the interdependence of the cultural and natural ecologies within which we live. Learning and pursuing truth for its own sake sounds noble and uplifting, especially in a world dominated by the language of those corporate and digital cultures that have discovered the virtue of hiring liberal education graduates because their critical thinking skills contribute to increased efficiency and the bottom line.

The more important question is whether courses in philosophy, history, and the other liberal arts will enable liberal arts graduates to recognize and resist how corporations and the digital revolution are colonizing other cultures and overshooting the sustaining capacity of the Earth's natural systems.

With a world population now moving beyond 7 billion people, with a global race to expand economies that put billions of tons of carbon dioxide into the atmosphere and into the world's oceans, and with the ongoing efforts to transform other cultures to fit the West's economic and technological agenda, to justify anything on the grounds of truth and learning for its own sake seems as divorced from reality as the abstract theories of mainstream philosophers and social theorists who are the basis of a liberal education. Before judging whether previous graduates of the country's elite universities such as Yale and Princeton, whose liberal arts programs closely approximate (at least in their promotional statements) Deresiewicz's ideal of pursuing truth and learning for its own sake, we need to ask: How many of their graduates sought careers with the CIA or Wall Street, and how many now head corporations that continue to deny that there is an ecological crisis?

The question to ask is whether a liberal arts education, as articulated by Deresiewicz, is relevant in today's world of deepening ecological crisis, a world undergoing irreversible change by scientists and technologists who are addicted to innovation but do not understand the cultures into which their innovations are being introduced. For them progress, like seeking truth and learning for its own sake, is self-justified—even if it leads to the total surveillance culture envisioned by Jeremy Bentham; even if it leads to machines replacing face-to-face relationships and reduces the need for workers; even if it promotes a monolithic mentality that relies upon the abstractions inherent in data and print-based representations.

A strong case can be made that the "instructional technologies" centered on the humanities reinforce the abstract thinking that marginalizes awareness of the emergent, relational, and linguistically diverse world we live in. The main contribution of mainstream Western philosophy, it can be argued, promoted abstract theory that degenerated into endless debates about issues that had little relevance to the social justice issues of their times or of our times. How different would our political world have been if they had given close attention to cultural traditions that strengthened community (and had a smaller adverse impact on natural systems), such as the diverse cultural commons and even such traditions as the craft guild systems?

The abstract theories of Plato, John Locke (especially his view on the origins of private property and the irrelevance of traditions), Adam Smith (who argued for free markets and against the protections and mutual support systems characteristic of the guild systems), René Descartes, Thomas Hobbes, Jeremy Bentham, and even John Dewey (a Social Darwinian thinker) were all based on ethnocentric thinking and a human-centered world. None understood the cultural differences between oral- and print-based thinking and cultural storage—including how the latter undermines the exercise of ecological intelligence. And none understood how the language community into which they were born reproduces the deep cultural assumptions that frame much of their metaphorical language, which in turn became the taken-for-granted basis of their thinking.

Does reading and debating the ideas of these philosophers lead to students understanding the cultural/linguistic roots of the ecological crisis? Given the silences and cultural biases in the liberal education of their professors, are they likely to engage students in a discussion of the differences between the views of intelligence promoted by mainstream philosophers and the ways that non-Western cultures exercise and encode in their languages the ecological intelligence of earlier generations? Are they likely to understand how the Enlightenment's narrow and historically specific examples of tradition have been transformed into an anti-tradition tradition of thinking that finds new ideas, values, and technologies (regardless of the traditions being overturned such as *habeas corpus,* personal privacy, and freedom from being hacked) actually represent *progress?* What forms of progress would be questioned by students engaged in the "instructional technologies" advocated by Deresiewicz?

Deresiewicz is correct in acknowledging that "building a self that is strong and creative and free" is not done in thin air, but by encountering ways that others have done so themselves (155). Yet when he puts forward those who should be studied for having addressed the basic questions of life, as he puts it, "questions of love, death, family, morality, time, truth, God, and everything else within the wide, starred universe of human experience" (156), he ignores one of their chief silences; namely, regarding how to live in mutually supportive communities that do not degrade the natural systems upon which all life depends.

I will return to this issue after identifying the silence he shares with others in the Western pantheon of humanists from whom students are to learn how to create themselves. His statement that a self, even an autonomous self (which is one of the fictions widely shared in Western cultures), is not built out of thin air, is basically correct. However, this process of identity and thought formation is one of the taken-for-granted ways that basic assumptions of the culture are intergenerationally passed forward through its layered metaphorical languages. That is, the history of the West can be understood as a history of metaphorical thinking, just as the histories and thus different epistemologies of other cultures can be understood as their own histories of metaphorical thinking, derived from profoundly different mythopoetic narratives. Philosophers, scientists, writers, performing artists, theologians, crafts-persons who combine skill with aesthetic judgment, bankers, patriots, and the myriad of people who exploit others—all rely upon different traditions of metaphorical thinking to explain to themselves and to others how they understand the world and what they hope to achieve.

This insight, as noted earlier, was central to Nietzsche's thinking about living in an interpreted world. But where in a liberal arts education would students acquire a deep understanding of the layered way their unquestioned vocabularies carry forward the meaning of words that were framed by analogs influenced by the root metaphors of earlier eras, when the myth of progress did not take account of environmental limits? How many liberal arts faculty learned from their mentors that the conduit view of language, which is essential to maintaining the myths of an individual's original ideas and objective knowledge, serves to hide that words have a history, and that the meanings were in many cases framed by analogs chosen in the past? How many can explain why the theory of metaphorical thinking of Mark Johnson and George Lakoff (1999) fails to take account of the deep cultural origins of metaphorical thinking that not only represents the colonization of the present by the past, but also our built environments?

Deresiewicz's failure to understand how a culture's ecology of language influences the formation of self-identity in ways that operate at pre-conscious levels of awareness is evident in how he explains the power of art and literature to provide models of who we want to be. As he puts it,

> The highest function of art, and of literature in particular, is to bring us to that knowledge of ourselves that college ought to start to give us. ... Art gives names to experience. We recognize Antigone or the Wife of Bath or Madame Bovary as permanent human types—the doomed idealist, the unabashed sensualist, the discontented dreamer–as well as permanent potentialities within ourselves. Think of the role that literary characters have played—Ahab, Huck Finn, Gatsby, Holden, Sethe—in articulating the American consciousness. (160–61)

There are a number of questions that need to be asked about whether any of these model individuals, perhaps with the exception of Gatsby, have affected the culture's impact on the land, on prioritizing greed and the unlimited accumulation of wealth that has contributed to so many social injustices, and on colonizing other cultures to adopt the American approach to modernization.

One of those questions is: Does learning from gifted authors, whose consciousness reflected earlier eras and social classes within different cultures, provide students real insight into who they are or who they want to become? Does it prepare them to recognize how the industrial/consumer-dependent lifestyle, and now the digital revolution, undermine face-to-face participation in cultural commons activities? These latter contribute to character formation that is profoundly different from the character formation that occurs in consumer relationships and in work settings that fit the requirements of an increasingly machine-driven economy. Deresiewicz also suggests that education should prepare students to "participate in that very rare thing in human history, collective self-government" (170). This is yet another example of how his own liberal arts education left him unaware of his ethnocentric thinking. Many indigenous cultures have a longer history of the democratic choice of their leaders, and in making decisions about their community's well-being.

Where does he explain how a liberal education is to address the silences in the education of most liberal arts faculty, such as how the digital revolution and corporate values have already undermined democratic decision-making? How many people are aware of the hard-won traditions they have already lost in the name of technological progress? We are beginning to understand how the digital revolution undermines long-term memory and intergenerational face-to-face communication, but how does it influence the process of self-creation that seems to be Deresiewicz's primary concern? What do young people learn about themselves from spending long hours looking at a computer screen, participating in social networks, and playing video games? Does Western literature and art (and which of the many periods of art?) prepare the next generation to understand that they may be the last generation to take on the challenge of slowing what some scientists now regard as the early stages of the 6th extinction of life on this Earth (Kolbert, 2014)? Educational reforms based on finding answers in a past that was unaware of environmental limits and ignorant of alternatives to an individualistic/consumer-dependent/industrial culture, can only lead further into the politics of escapism. Unlike other groups engaged in the politics of denial, such as the promoters of free markets and unending technological progress, liberal arts graduates and faculty can claim the higher values of pursuing knowledge for its own sake.

RESCUING THE LIBERAL ARTS FROM FACULTIES IN DENIAL

There is double bind that must be addressed if Deresiewicz's escapist version of a liberal arts education is to be avoided. The double bind is that the knowledge that provides a basis for recognizing how to make a liberal arts education relevant in the ecologically stressed 21st century is the very knowledge that has been relegated as too low-status and therefore not included in the curriculum, as well as relegated to the margins of different disciplines. The former includes the intergenerational knowledge, skills, and mentoring that are the basis of the world's diverse cultural commons (which will be discussed in greater depth in the next chapter). The knowledge that still exists on the margins of different disciplines includes the fields of (i) eco-lingustics, which encompasses the literature on the differences between orality and literacy, as well as the ecology of metaphorical language; (ii) the sociology of knowledge, which clarifies the role of language in constituting what becomes a person's reality; (iii) literature that focuses on the culture-mediating characteristics of technology, and (iv) the thinking of Gregory Bateson and Alfred North Whitehead. These last two provide the conceptual basis for recognizing how the emergent, relational, and co-dependent nature of the cultural and natural ecologies within which we live are marginalized by the romantic focus on individual self-discovery and creation.

This double bind could be addressed if current liberal arts faculty took the ecological crisis seriously enough to place a moratorium on their current research until they acquired the basic insights of these diverse yet closely related fields of knowledge. But this is unlikely to happen on the scale that is needed. For the few liberal arts faculty who view the ecological crisis as serious enough to change their immediate career priorities, and for students who are more likely to be concerned about how the ecological crisis, the digital revolution, and the prospect of continual global warfare, I will suggest a few ways in which the liberal arts can become more relevant to understanding the dominant forces shaping the 21st century.

The starting point in the long march toward ecologically sustainable thinking is to read the most prominent Western philosophers in a way that prioritizes the questions most relevant to our 21st century experience, rather than debating the answers to the questions they posed. For example, nearly all the major philosophers were abstract theorists who relied upon the technology of print. Did they understand that print is inherently ethnocentric? Has this tradition of cultural storage and thinking influenced our assumptions that print-based cultural storage and thinking are more reliable than face-to-face communication? Did their ethnocentrism creep into the list of the 100 Great Books promoted by Mortimer Adler and considered by many to be essential to a liberal education? Were their debates about the sources of knowledge and values ever informed by ethnographic descriptions of different cultural groups' practices—or were they so habituated to abstract thinking that it never occurred to them that questions relevant to future generations would relate to the beliefs, practices, and values that contributed to morally coherent and mutually supportive communities—which differ from culture to culture?

Many of these abstract and culturally indifferent theorists lived at a time when their environment was being degraded to the point where the discovery of the "New World" (to use the ethnocentric metaphors of their era) made possible the continuation of living by their ecologically uninformed ways of thinking. I know the criticism will be made that awareness of ecological systems occurred only in the last 150 or so years in the West. However, indigenous cultures—some going back 8000 years in the case of the Inca (now Quechua) and between 40,000 and 50,000 years in the case of the Australian Aboriginal people—exercised ecological intelligence in adapting their cultural practices to the cycles and patterns of the land. The central question to be asked in reading the theories of key Western philosophers is: What traditions of thinking did they initiate that continue to limit our understanding of how abstract thinking and its supporting technologies undermine the exercise of ecological intelligence? Silence, to recall Foucault's insight about the exercise of power, is also an action upon an action that leads to ignoring what should have been debated before committing ourselves to an uncritical acceptance of print-based cultural storage and thinking.

Literary criticism has taken many forms in the past, but its varied ways of raising questions about the unquestioned world of culture (including social injustices) does not fit Deresiewicz's understanding of personal discovery and self-creation. There is a deeper level at which language organizes and carries forward the misconceptions and silences from the past. These need to be explored in any encounter with literature, even in oral traditions. That is, the myth that represents written and spoken language-based communication as operating as a sender/ receiver process, or as what Michael Reddy (1979) referred to as a conduit view of communication, reinforces the myth that words refer to real entities, and that they convey the ideas or thoughts of the person who uses them. This process has served to hide the metaphorical nature of most words. As I have explained earlier, the meaning of most of our vocabulary—such as "individual," "intelligence," "liberal," "tradition," "data," "science," and so forth—were framed by analogs settled upon in earlier times. For example, the choice of analogs that framed the meaning of the word "woman" reflected the misconceptions and prejudices of earlier times. Words, to reiterate a key point, have a history, and when we are born into an existing cultural ecology of language, our level of intelligence too often is limited by the level of intelligence that is encoded in the metaphorical language that is passed forward and taken for granted as reality.

George Lakoff and Mark Johnson produced a highly useful though introductory explanation of the pervasiveness of metaphorical thinking in *Metaphors We Live By* (1980). However, the gravitational pull of gaining respectability within the field of cognitive science led them to update their explanation of metaphorical thinking. In *Philosophy in the Flesh*, they argued that the origin of the analogs that frame the meaning of words are derived from embodied experiences. As they put it,

> Conceptualization Only Through the Body: We can only form concepts through the body. Therefore, every understanding that we can have of the world, ourselves, and others can only be formed in terms of concepts shaped by our bodies. (1999, 555).

In short, the analogs for understanding such metaphors as up and down, forward and backward, tall and short, full and empty, are derived from bodily experiences. Yes, this is partly correct, just as the old system of measurement such as inches, yards, and miles, provided the analogs derived from bodily experiences. But their view of metaphor excludes the possibility that the analogs that framed the current meaning of such words as "tradition," "data," "individualism," "woman," and so forth have a history. In learning to use these words without questioning the historically derived analogs that continue to frame their meanings, the individual reproduces earlier forms of thinking, including the earlier misconceptions. Their emphasis on the brain/embodied origin of the analogs that frame the meaning of words also fails to take account of how other cultures undergo a process of colonization when they integrate into their daily vocabularies such words as "progress," "individualism," "modern," "development," and so on.

One of the ironies is that the field of cognitive science locates mental activities as occurring only in the brain where the behavior of neurons can be observed and measured. Like the Johnson/Lakoff theory of the embodied nature of metaphorical thinking, the presence of metaphorical thinking throughout the multiple communication patterns in the cultural ecologies—in people's clothes, patterns of metacommunication, design of buildings and layout of physical space, and creative arts such as music and dance—are ignored. Again, we see how understanding cultural and natural ecologies is limited by reducing intelligence to what occurs in the brain. The reductionist thinking required by the scientific method relies upon a mechanistic interpretive framework that, in effect, dictates that if a thing cannot be empirically observed and measured, it does not exist. Thus, the role of metaphorical thinking in the semiotic systems of cultures, as well as the role these systems play in natural systems, becomes another one of the silences in today's politics. What cannot be measured by magnetic resonance imaging (MRI) and other technologies does not exist. This is yet another example of how ideology (in this case the hegemony of the root metaphor of mechanism and the scientific method) limits understanding the languaging processes of a culture such that what should be part of the political discourse, is not. Just as the Johnson/Lakoff theory of metaphor precludes understanding the destructive effects of linguistic colonization, it also limits understanding the Orwellian misuse of political metaphors such as conservatism, free markets, and progress.

The history of a culture's vocabularies has important implications for all areas of the liberal arts. If the the myth of the autonomous individual is to be overcome, then one must, from a historical and cross-cultural perspective, question the origins of the analogs taken for granted by the author, artist, scientist, and philosopher. What are the analogs that John Locke assumes when he uses the word "property," or that René Descartes assumes when he claims we can live without historical knowledge? What was taken for granted when the idea of progress as a linear movement into the future became widely used? What were the deep cultural influences that led Francis Bacon (1561–1626), Johannes Kepler (1571–1630), and Thomas Hobbes (1588–1679) to plant deeply in mainstream Western consciousness the idea that biological processes and political behavior exhibit machine-like characteristics? The taken-for-granted metaphorical vocabulary of the historian, philosopher, and social theorist, and writers such as Kafka and Camus, also need to be examined for what they reveal about the deep cultural assumptions being carried forward in their writings. Giving attention to the cultural epistemology encoded in metaphorical language will provide a better understanding of why the liberal arts have been so slow to recognize the cultural/linguistic roots of the ecological crisis—or that, in the case of many faculty, that there is a crisis.

The presupposed metaphorical language within one discipline serves as a barrier to understanding the metaphorical languages used by other disciplines. Thus we can now see how difficult it is for highly educated people to recognize that print and data represent a static and abstract world—one that differs from process-oriented thinkers such as Gregory Bateson and Alfred North Whitehead. These two understood everyday reality as emergent, relational, co-dependent. Bateson, for example, was particularly clear about the dangers of relying upon an inherited metaphorical language that limits awareness of bio- and eco-semiotically coded messages pertaining to the changes occuring in natural systems. Giving more eco-linguistically sensitive attention to how writers unknowingly reproduce the deep assumptions of their culture has a utility that goes beyond seeking truth for its own sake. It may lead to an awareness that our increasingly unsustainable lifestyle can only be rectified by correcting the misconceptions carried forward in vocabularies we otherwise take for granted. Approaching the liberal arts by reproducing the romantic thinking of Deresiewicz, and the many liberal arts faculty who share his way of thinking, undermines the possibility of a political discourse focusing on ecologically sustainable thinking. There are, indeed, more profound issues today than self-discovery and modeling one's life on Huck Finn or Holden Caulfield.

There is another way to approach the liberal arts. If self-discovery and self-transformation are goals of a liberal education, then the actual process of acquiring these skills and practicing the various arts would be more transformative than reading about an artist's life and discussing the influences that shaped her or his work. An emphasis on praxis does not, of course, eliminate the importance of reading and learning how others addressed the basic existential issues of their day. However, reading about and discussing the lives of creative people has a less transformative effect than being mentored in one of the performing or visual arts.

This approach will also add to self-understanding, but, more importantly, it will be essential to learning how to mentor coming generations. Best of all, turning discussion sessions into the development of an actual talent as an artist or craftsperson leads to a more community-centered life; one that has a smaller adverse ecological impact. This should be the goal of a liberal arts education, but it is one that Deresiewicz does not mention. How this lifestyle is strengthened by participating with others in renewing the cultural commons rather than engaging in deep discussions that are nevertheless still abstract will be the focus of Chapter Seven.

❧ 6 ❧

Wisdom Traditions: Another Silence
Perpetuated by Universities

IN ASSESSING THE ECOLOGICALLY DESTRUCTIVE PATH that universities have put us on, we need to ask: Has their promotion of the authority of objective knowledge and data consigned wisdom to the junk-heap of history? Has the digital revolution now made these traditions totally irrelevant? Unlike earlier technologies, the digital revolution is producing profound changes, only partially understood, in the world's cultures. The unique thing about these changes is that they are embraced by many people, ranging from scientists to business people, educators, average citizens, and just about everybody else who values convenience, instantaneousness, multiple forms of apparent empowerment, and the ability to escape from face-to-face relationships into the seemingly boundless world of data. The combination of surveillance technologies — connectivity, multiple monitoring systems, and storage — brings all aspects of the natural world, as well as cultural life, under the new God of capitalism and "rational" data-based decision-making. Quickly disappearing from human memory are the various mythologically centered gods that provided an integrated and morally coherent worldview. This worldview was renewed through rituals and narratives, and in many instances, prescribed punishments fitted to different moral transgressions. There are extreme reactionary movements now resisting how these ancient belief systems are being replaced by the new God of data and rational decision-making. This only strengthens the resolve of the elites guiding this new religion to marginalize the voices of those who resist being converted to the modern, secular, and data-based understanding of the emerging world.

While this new God and its new priesthood have not totally displaced the God of the Old and New Testaments, the emphasis of the new religion upon the authority of data is bringing about fundamental changes in the past vocabularies cultures used to carry forward their wisdom traditions. For those closest to the center of this digital revolution, the word "wisdom" is seldom, if ever, used. When Bill Gates, an early prophet of this new religion, purportedly claimed that we need to recover wisdom, few people would have known what the word used to mean. And few know what it might mean in the modern world where data is understood as eliminating subjective judgments and interpretations based on archaic moral narratives. The vision of 17th and 18th century Enlightenment philosophers is at last being realized by computer scientists who now put decision-making on a so-called objective basis that relies upon data. The authority of objective knowledge, information, and now data even transcends the murky realm of politics, which is too often influenced by memory and values derived from the pre-scientific world of ancient religious narratives.

Those who refuse to recognize the authority of data are still looking through a glass darkly. This archaic mindset leads to raising questions for which there are no objective answers — such as the differences between wisdom and data. Taking seriously the differences would require entering a realm already colonized by the followers of the scientific method who have demonstrated the power to predict the behavior of particles moving through space.

The astonishing achievements of scientists suggest that we do not need to understand wisdom. What can wisdom help us understand if science has given us the ability to land men on the moon and to genetically alter different forms of life? Besides, understanding wisdom first requires understanding the diversity of how humans have understood the nature and sources of wisdom. And what citizen of the digital age can take time away from tweets, cell phones, and e-mail from friends and employers—especially when the latter expect their employees to be continually connected? And who is interested in entering the rabbit hole of human history (chronicled by the winners), and who is genuinely concerned that the abstract world of data misrepresents the emergent, relational, co-dependent life-sustaining processes of the natural and cultural ecologies within which we live? Isn't it enough that data can be used to reveal trend lines in profits, the expansion or reduction in crime rates, and the rate of acidification of the world oceans?

There is no question that the abstract world of data is genuinely useful, even when it represents a formulaic response that hides the many limitations of what data is supposed to represent, even when the moral consequences of political decisions are concealed in its use. As the above sentences suggest, moving outside the certainties of an objective and measurable world requires understanding that one's thinking is based on a culturally specific, taken-for-granted ontology. It requires recognizing that this is a culturally constructed world, the basic ideas of which are *assumptions*—for example, (i) that this world is composed of fixed entities, such as autonomous individuals and abstract ideas; (ii) that values are universal and objective; (iii) that there is life force called progress, which is like a road sign pointing in the direction the rest of the world is to follow.

Recognizing the conceptual foundations of one's own taken-for-granted ontology seems like an unnecessary detour when data are so easy to understand. Why search for an alternative—an ontology that avoids colonization because it recognizes that all life-forming and sustaining processes, across the entire range of natural and cultural systems, are emergent, relational, co-dependent, and sustained by different ecologies of communication? This would require more than historical knowledge. That is, it would require a knowledge of other cultures—especially those that recognize an emergent, relational, and co-dependent world as the basis of ecological intelligence. For the typical citizen of the emerging digital culture, this effort would seem to be a waste of time. After all, the new class of experts, the data scientists, as well as the computer scientists, programmers, and engineers working behind the scenes to create autonomous algorithms, possess a form of intelligence that easily turns data into decisions.

THE TAKEN-FOR-GRANTED ONTOLOGY
OF THE WORLD OF DATA

Before discussing why wisdom is needed in a world that increasingly relies on data-based decision-making, as well as how data misrepresents the world we live in, it must be acknowledged that, for all its limitations, data is useful in providing a better understanding of patterns, trends, casual relationships, rates of change, and changes in effectiveness and efficiency. It provides, in many instances, a more accurate account of the behavior of social and natural systems that might otherwise be misrepresented from (i) lack of close attention, or (ii) efforts to hide the shortcomings of human behavior. For example, without data we have to rely upon conjecture and traditional misconceptions about the behavior of marine ecosystems. Data provides a more accurate understanding of how many sharks are being killed each year in order to satisfy a traditional cultural preference for shark fin soup. Similarly, data provides a more accurate understanding of how fraudulent Medicare and Social Security claims are distorting the national budget. Data is also useful in providing an expanded understanding of other cultural patterns of behavior relating to gender and racial discrimination, and so forth.

In spite of its many uses, data, like the scientific method, tells us "what is" within a limited context. It does not tell us how we "ought" to respond to the issues and problems revealed by the "what is" information. In order to understand the limitations of data and the role of cultural influences — largely ignored due to an over estimation of the authority conferred on data — it is necessary to take account of the following:

1.   Like print, unexamined cultural assumptions influence both what is presumed as important to represent in the form of data, as well as the interpretation of how that data is to be used. That is, while data

is assumed to be objective, there is always a decision made by an individual or group about what is to be measured and represented as data. This decision is culturally influenced because the thinking and values of decision makers are influenced by the languaging processes that tacitly reproduce earlier cultural ways of thinking and valuing. As data represents only a segment, like a snapshot, of what is emergent, relational, and co-dependent within the larger ecological system, what it represents (like René Magritte's famous painting "Ceci n'est pas une pipe") is only a partial, abstract, and symbolic image. (It is an *image* of the pipe; not the pipe itself.) In short, data is only a surface representation, and it encodes the assumptions that initially influence decisions about what data is to be collected.

2. How the data is interpreted is also a culturally influenced process. The mindset of the individual and/or group interpreting the data is always under the influence of the cultural assumptions that are taken for granted. For example, the environmental scientist brings a different set of assumptions and values to the process of interpreting data than the scientists working for a corporation or an office of education concerned with acquiring "objective" evidence of "learning outcomes." What the myth of objective data requires overlooking is the ecology of linguistic influences, the ecology of identities, and the ecology of interpretative and moral frameworks that are variously called an ideology, the scientific method, and the individual's critical rationality. The cultural/linguistic ecology that influences both ends of the data collecting and interpreting process are inescapable aspects of the interpreted world in which we live. That we can escape into a world of objective facts, data, and printed words is a modern myth.

3. Because the surface and momentary measurement or observation of a phenomenon does not take into account its larger dynamic context, and because many Westerners carry forward the Cartesian tradition of thinking of themselves as rational spectators of an inert, material, external world, data (as well as print) reinforces a basic

ontological misconception about a world of permanent, fixed, and Platonic universals, and thus abstract entities. Those who claim to have a rational and thus objective understanding of this abstract world too often possess power and authority over those who acknowledge they live in an impermanent and interpreted world.

4. The ideology that serves as an interpretive framework for determining the meaning and uses of data reinforces an instrumental moral framework that, with the exception of how environmentalists use data, serves the interests of market liberals who promote consumerism and the monetization of everyday life. This instrumental moral framework is supported by the cultural assumptions about the autonomy of the individual and the importance of progress in producing material wealth and in exploiting the environment.

It would not be too much of a stretch to claim that the dominant Anglo/European print-based culture, out of ignorance of its own modernizing assumptions, uses data as though it legitimates the decisions that lead to further economic progress. That is, data is being viewed as providing both an account of "what is" as well as what "ought to be." Actually, what is represented as data is too limited, and too much a reflection of the assumptions of the experts who initiate the data gathering in the first place, and who provide the moral guidelines for how it is to be used. Moral and instrumental guidelines are derived, instead, from the prevailing ideology of the social groups seeking legitimation for their decisions. If people were to recognize the ideology of the groups masking their policy decisions, including the justifications for replacing people with machines, they might challenge these ideologies more often. But how many people have been educated to recognize how certain words in the vocabulary, such as "objective," "rational," "progress," "expert," "science," and now "data," are assumed to represent certainties that are beyond political debate. The irony is that when judged in terms of past decisions made by ideologically driven groups who have relied on data to justify their economic and political agendas, data-based decision-making has been both de-humanizing as well as ecologically destructive. This is true whether it has been in promoting technological innovations, in monetizing the cultural commons, in colonizing other cultures, and in educating the country's youth to equate success and happiness with consumerism and wasteful living. Indeed, data has become the common currency shared by the interlocking surveillance technologies that are putting the country on the road to a techno-fascist future.

If current market and individually centered ideologies are accelerating environmental changes that are leading to the planet's 6th mass extinction (as some scientists believe), then the recovery of wisdom traditions becomes not only more relevant but more urgent. When we consider not only the wisdom traditions within different cultures, but also how these traditions were influenced by profoundly different cultural mythologies and epistemologies—centuries of learning how to encode their guiding moral frameworks into narratives, dance, and every aspect of their cultural commons, as well as their relationships with the natural world—then the only question becomes not whether these traditions can lead to fundamental changes in the Western mindset, but whether they can be learned in time to avert the social chaos and ecological endgame that lies just decades ahead.

In spite of my increasing doubts that the majority of academics and experts who are guiding reform agendas will take seriously the challenge of basing decisions on wisdom rather than data, I will nevertheless identify a number of wisdom traditions that still guide human/nature relationships. These are the traditions from which those who are resisting the mainstream individualistic, consumer-dependent, and profit-oriented culture are learning.

TWO ANCIENT, RELATIONALLY ORIENTED WISDOM TRADITIONS: BUDDHISM AND CONFUCIANISM

The fundamental difference between wisdom traditions and cultural patterns reinforced by data-based storage, thinking, and communication can be seen by comparing what Buddhists call the Path with what they call "wondering about." This latter phrase refers to a life that is not reflective, that is continually influenced by outside forces and shifting subjective whims. "Wondering about" is exemplified in the West by a consumer-driven lifestyle and the many illnesses that accompany it. It is bolstered by how the Internet reinforces change, short attention spans and memory, and an instrumental approach to information and data.

The Path, on the other hand, leads to a life of mindfulness and thus to a radical transformation in life's guiding principles. The names of the Path's eight steps includes the following: (1) right views, (2) right intent, (3) right speech, (4) right conduct, (5) right livelihood, (6) right effort, (7) right mindfulness, (8) right concentration (Smith, 1991, 105–12). It is notable that possessing the right amount of data is not included as contributing to the path of mindfulness. As the behavioral and thought process associated with each of these steps is elaborated upon, it becomes clear that Buddhism is focused on the moral and spiritual dimensions of relationships as they are experienced in a constantly changing world. It is also clear that the Path requires a lifelong commitment, which differs radically from the short attention span and expectation of obtaining instantaneous results reinforced by cyberspace experiences. Perhaps more important in terms of the need to reduce human impact on natural systems, the Path represents an alternative to the consumer-dependent lifestyle valued in the West. It is also important to note that different traditions of Buddhism are being taken seriously in the West, but not in sufficient numbers to have a real impact on the still growing influence of the digital revolution that supports global expansion of the market system.

Confucianism, like Buddhism, is also a religion so deeply ingrained in daily cultural practices that it is understood more as the taken-for-granted reality of daily life. Its five-fold principles are as follows. *Jen* "involves simultaneously a feeling of humanity toward others and respect for oneself, an indivisible sense of the dignity of life wherever it appears." *Chun tzu* highlights relationships that are the opposite of the competitive, petty, and ego-centered person. The person of *Chun tzu* puts others at ease and engages in what Martin Buber later referred to as I-Thou relationships and dialogue. *Li* is the quality that leads to doing things correctly — in the use of language, in avoiding extremes, in the correct ordering of relationships within the family and society. *Te* is the power of moral example that attracts the willing support of the people. *Wen* refers to the "arts of peace," specifically the power of the arts to transform human nature in ennobling ways (Smith, 1991, 175–81). There is no mention of the importance of data in these life-guiding principles. But the digital revolution, which is central to economic growth in China and other cultures with a Confucian past, is having a transformative impact on the youth of these cultures.

A critical issue is whether the wisdom traditions of Buddhism and Confucianism will survive, as the mindset of youth in these cultures is being re-shaped by the Westernizing mindset of the digital revolution. The relational wisdom of both Buddhism and Confucianism was intergenerationally renewed though face-to-face communication, through mentoring, and through the knowledge that others took for granted these principles as moral imperatives. The spread of market forces, rising material standards of living, slick media images connecting consumerism with individual happiness, as well as the role of the digital revolution in expanding the economies of Asian countries and westernizing their approach to education, all work against youth even being aware of these ancient wisdom traditions—except to view them as the old and pre-modern ways of their grandparents.

ECOLOGICALLY INFORMED WISDOM TRADITIONS THAT ARE SOURCES OF RESISTANCE TO THE INDIVIDUALLY CENTERED, CONSUMER-DEPENDENT, AND DATA-BASED CULTURE

The ecologically informed wisdom traditions that stand in sharpest contrast to the Western mindset, and that have the most relevance for learning to live less environmentally destructive lives, are represented by the world's indigenous cultures. Their wisdom was not acquired from abstract thinkers such as Western philosophers, nor was it acquired from data or books. Rather, is was acquired from living in one place over hundreds, even thousands, of years—giving close attention to the cycles, patterns, and interdependencies of life in the natural world; using myths as repositories of practical, ecologically informed knowledge; narratives and ceremonies that wove generations into webs of meaning;

rituals around food and healing practices; and renewing the knowledge and moral insights learned from previous generations by taking account of the ongoing changes in the local bioregion. What seems common to these wisdom traditions is that, unlike the mythic account of "man's" fall, in Genesis, and the injunction to name and subordinate the plants and animals to human will, they learned from nature itself (or, the "Garden of Eden," to stay with that metaphor). That is, rather than escaping from the Garden by creating a human-centered world of moral and conceptual dichotomies and categories, indigenous cultures engaged in what is today known as biomimicry, and which shows up in their metaphorical language and knowledge of local ecosystems.

Giving close attention to information flowing within and between natural systems, such as how animal behavior and trees anticipate the severity of the coming winter, fosters reliance upon ecological intelligence. Awareness of the interconnected patterns in a world of impermanence, awareness of how to adapt human needs to this dynamic world in order to sustain life within the biotic/human community—these things are profoundly different from the surface, abstract, snapshot images we call data. There is no sense of the sacred in a world reproduced as data; there is no awareness of an inclusive spirituality. Without a sense of the sacred and an inclusive spirituality—when the cultural and natural worlds are reduced to data—then anything becomes possible, including destroying forests, mountains, streams—and the animals that inhabit them—if it leads to more profit and human conveniences.

The mythic thinking of the peoples who have inhabited the Andes for centuries, and whose understanding of Pachamama as the force that nurtures humans, even as humans nurture nature, has led to one of the world's mega-diversities of edible plants. It also represents many of the elements of wisdom shared by other indigenous cultures. As explained by Grimaldo Rengifo Vasquez,

> In the Andean world everything is alive and important; nothing is inert and nothing is superfluous. The very stone is alive, it speaks and the peasant converses with it as person to person. It is not that the peasant extends the notion of a person to the stone (which is generally understood as 'personification') but

rather that, for the peasant, the stone is alive—possessing the attributes of the *runa* and vice versa.

In the Andean context we cannot speak either of the inanimate as opposed to the animate, or of the essential as opposed to the contingent. The whole *Pacha* is a community of interconnected living being, in which man and water are as important and alive as are the *buacas* (deities) and the wind in terms of the regeneration of life. (Marglin, 1998, 97)

During my visit to Cajamarca, the site of Pizarro's capture and execution of Atahualpa, the sovereign emperor of the Inca empire, my Western consciousness was opened up to how the stone could be understood as being alive and an active participant in the information networks that connect all forms of life in the bioregion to the cosmos. My Western consciousness, oriented toward actions that increase efficiency and a humanly controlled world, led to wondering why the stones were not used as boundary markers, as in England, France, and other Western countries. Instead they lay scattered across the field. Following the advice to pick up a stone, I found how its surface appearance indicates the level of moisture in the soil, which is vital information for the farmer to understand. The number of eggs a bird lays, the number of animals in a herd, —even the condition of their fur— are signs of the current and forthcoming patterns operating in the regeneration of life. In effect, the wisdom carried forward from earlier centuries among the Andean peoples is that everything communicates, everything is part of the same spiritual and moral universe, and that these cycles of interdependence should not be broken. But now they *are* being broken, as Western extraction industries are tearing up the earth for oil, gold, and other resources needed to produce the throw-away, data-driven culture of the West.

Another example is the Aboriginal peoples who mapped and storied what we now call Australia for 40 to 50 thousand years. Their oral wisdom contrasts with the anthropocentrism of tribal cultures who transformed their narratives into print (which we know as the biblical book of Genesis). As recounted by Robert Lawlor in *Voices of the First Day: Awakening in the Aboriginal Dreamtime* (1991), Aboriginal cosmology was also the basis of their moral order. It provided the wisdom that guided their uses of technologies and resulted in a level of ecological intelligence that far surpassed the Anglo culture that invaded the land and set out to westernize them. Lawlor summarizes the wisdom that was integral to their cosmology in the following way:

> All creatures—from stars to humans to insects—share in the consciousness of the primary creative force, and each, in its own ways, mirrors a form of that consciousness. In this sense the Dreamtime stories perpetuate a unified worldview. This unity compelled the Aborigines to respect and adore the earth as if it were a book imprinted with the mystery of the original creation. The goal of life was to preserve the earth, as much as possible, in its initial purity. The subjugation and domestication of plants and animals and all the other manipulation and exploitation of the natural world—the basis of Western civilization and 'progress'—were antithetical to the sense of a common consciousness and origin shared by every creature and equally with the creators. To exploit this integrated world was to do the same to oneself. (17)

The cosmologies of the Quechua, the Australian Aborigine, as well as many other indigenous cultures, recognized a sacred and thus moral order that was (and is) profoundly different from the instructions in Genesis for man to name the creatures of God's creation and take control of them. What is often not recognized is that the Hebrew Bible was written by a tribal culture dedicated to a cosmology and moral order centered on a monotheistic God. The surrounding cultures that understood all forms of life as sacred and animated by different spirits, and thus as participants in the same spiritual universe, were regarded as challenging the one true God. The irony is that these first indigenous cultures initially pursued a path leading to ecological wisdom, while Genesis was interpreted to have laid out the conceptual and moral foundations of the anthropocentic culture of the West, which become the foundation of the industrial and capitalist exploitation of nature. This anthropocentric cosmology, as well as early biblical injunctions to take control of the earth and multiply (both contributing to the present ecological catastrophe), continues as the basis of today's emphasis on data-driven ideas of progress.

The youth of these indigenous cultures, from the Haida, Dene, and Inuit, to the thousands of other indigenous cultures spread around the world, are now caught between their ancient, ecologically informed sources of wisdom and the modern world of atomic individualism, consumerism, and the abstractions appearing on computer screens. The tension between time-tested forms of wisdom and the convenience of immediate access to data (generated by experts whose long-range goal is to replace much of what is human with robots and machine forms of intelligence), is clearly articulated by a young woman who is herself caught between the two worlds. While pursuing a graduate degree at the University of Hawaii, she writes about the cosmology that is a source of ecological wisdom, and how it is being threatened by the modern world's pursuit of progress. As she put it:

> *He aliʻi ka ʻāina, he kauwā ke kanaka* (the land is a chief, man is the servant) is a wise saying in our traditions. *ʻĀina* encompasses the land, sky, ocean and all contained therein including plants, animals, and that which feeds and nourishes life. Our role as *Kanaka ʻŌiwi* ("Hawaiians") is found in the genealogical relationship and responsibility to that which preceded us — plants/animals, our islands, the soils and waters that feed the plants/animals, to the eldest of the elements. Our responsibility extends to those who will come after us, our children and future generations. Our elders past say they are buried and they in turn become of the land. So we actively care for and protect our *ʻāina* out of gratitude and survival because it feeds us physically; when we return to nurture and be nurtured by the *ʻāina* it feeds us spiritually by restoring ancestral memory. Our ancestral wisdom/memory/traditions are alive today in our *ʻāina,* in our elders, in our language, in our chants and song, in our *naʻau* (where your navel is, your *naʻau* are your guts, your soul).

> One of our beloved elders Pualani Kanahele reminds us all "I am this land, and this land is me." We perpetuate the love and respect our ancestors shared with their specific lands by telling

their stories, continuing to grow native cultivars of taro, fighting for our waters and the inherent right to use them, through education — teaching our young, hands and feet in the soil and waters. We have a saying that is being used politically at the moment in protest to the building of telescopes on top our sacred mountains: "until the very last Aloha 'Āina." We will stand and ensure the continuity of our place and knowledge until the very last being that protects our land — through persistence, truth, and aloha. (Personal communication, 9/1/15)

Where — in the narratives of the computer scientists, of data scientists, of heads of corporations, of agencies protecting the nation's security, and of all the other individuals and groups that have now made data the highest form of knowledge — do we find any concern about the lack of ecologically informed wisdom, such as that articulated in the above observations? What is being lost? The most abstract (that is context-free) bits of information that are constructed on the basis of some expert's cultural assumptions — one who is often working for others higher up in the system of economic and human exploitation — are supposed to guide decisions that will impact people's lives. People are largely unaware of the shortcomings of this data and the various ideologies that guide its use. One of the great ironies of our time is that the ecologically informed wisdom traditions are relegated to the margins of the higher education system. These are the anthropology courses that teach students about the "backwardness" of pre-rational cultures that are still guided by story telling myths.

The other irony, for which everyone will pay dearly as ecological systems begin to collapse, is that the possibility of finding the basis of an ecologically or even relationally informed wisdom tradition in our own Western culture is being undermined by the values and knowledge given higher status in our public schools and universities. As I observed in an earlier book, *The Culture of Denial* (1997), the high-status knowledge being promoted in higher education is largely print-based and thus abstract. Increasingly, it is also computer mediated. This knowledge was ideologically framed by the misconceptions of 17th century Enlightenment thinkers who promoted overturning traditions and relying instead upon critical thinking, scientific knowledge, and a secular worldview. Central to the high-status knowledge promoted in higher education are deep cultural assumptions about (i) the autonomous nature of the individual, (ii) a mechanistic and human-centered (anthropocentric) world, (iii) the progressive nature of change, and (iv) the combination of cultural hubris and missionary spirit that justifies colonizing other cultures to adopt these core features of the Western mindset. Given the characteristics of high-status knowledge, and the increasing reliance upon computer-mediated thinking and entertainment, there is little likelihood that either students or their professors will even be aware of the relational wisdom of Buddhism and Confucianism, or the ecologically informed wisdom traditions of indigenous cultures. The Western university may not see it, but indigenous peoples are increasing aware of how Western culture is accelerating the global changes threatening their future existence.

In recent decades, environmentally concerned scholars of Judaism and Christianity have questioned the long-held interpretations of Genesis, but, in spite of that, its established anthropocentric message continues to influence the consciousness of most Jews, Christians (especially fundamentalist Christians), and even the growing number of atheists. These latter adhere to more of the Judeo/Christian cosmology than they realize. And there are writers such as Henry David Thoreau, Aldo Leopold, Rachel Carson, and Wendell Berry who provide key sensitivities and insights upon which a wisdom tradition could be based, but will youth encounter their work as they search the Internet? And if they were to discover any of them, each student would still need to make her/his own decision about taking such writers seriously when contrasted with the consumer-oriented cultural ecology that impinges on their senses and communicates a different message: namely, that consumerism is still the main road to personal happiness and success. Data is the basis of this message, and the basis, too, of innovations that will keep the economy expanding while simultaneously shrinking opportunities to work in settings not dictated by digital systems.

We need to decide whether to allow our decisions about the natural world to be guided by wisdom traditions or driven by data. Perhaps the final blow to the hope of allowing a wisdom tradition to guide us is that few people, even those who are highly educated, understand what is problematic about the origin and uses of data. It has now acquired a cult standing, which will only be strengthened as the digital revolution expands its influence over more aspects of daily life.

The final judgment is that wisdom within the context of Western culture is still viewed as an obstacle to a historically dominant message of Genesis, which is: "Be fruitful, and multiply, and replentish the earth, and subdue it: and have dominion over the fish of the sea, and over the fowl of the air, and over everything that moveth upon the earth (Genesis 1:28). Computer scientists have announced that the transition to the age of singularity is now occurring, and that super-intelligent computers will take over as the world enters the post-biological phase of evolution. In other words, it will be up to computers to interpret what "dominion" means, and whether the wisdom of the myth-tellers should guide their use of data.

REFERENCES

Holy Bible, King James Version.

Bowers, Chet, *The Culture of Denial* (1997)

Lawlor, R. 1991. *Voices of the First Day: Awakening in the Aboriginal Dreamtime.* Rochester, VT. Inner Traditions International.

Rengifo, Vasquez, G. 1998. "The AYLLU." In *The Spirit of Regeneration: Andean Culture Confronting Western Notions of Development.* London: Zed Books.

Smith, H. 1991. *The World's Religions.* New York: Harper One.

ᐅ 7 ᐊ

The Cultural Commons as Sustainable Pathways in an Increasingly Stressed World

IT IS AS THOUGH THE LIMITED THINKING of our ancestors still encoded in our everyday vocabularies prevents us from recognizing the relational nature of the world in which we live. Recent opinion polls have found that over 60 percent of the American public is concerned about climate change—and with the extreme weather being experienced in different parts of the country, this figure is likely to go up. Pope Francis' encyclical, *Laudato Si'* presents the moral arguments for taking seriously the science of climate change. It identifies neoliberal market ideology and the industrial approach to progress as chiefly responsible for the environmental degradation now having the greatest impact on the poor, and it will likely influence political debates around the world. But unlike the shifts in public awareness revealed in recent polls, the related questions are not being raised; namely, how to promote community-centered alternatives to the West's continuing emphasis on consumerism and growing the economy. It's as though adopting new technologies that reduce greenhouse gases will solve the problem, letting people get back to their normal consumer-dependent lifestyles.

On the cultural margins of industrialized cultures, as well as within many non-Western cultures, the intergenerational knowledge and skills that sustained the cultural commons are being increasingly recognized as the only viable alternative to the fossil fuel and consumer-dependent culture. As these expressions of life-sustaining localism movements do not receive the media exposure given to crime, financial emergencies, political debates, and larger-than-life personalities, the cultural pathways that represent the most viable alternative to ecological catastrophe do not become part of the conversation about reducing greenhouse gases.

These local, ecologically sustainable lifestyles can be supported by people simply deciding to move from their habitul consumerism to a fuller engagement in the cultural commons that exist in every community. But becoming more involved in the largely non-monetized activities of the cultural commons does not mean returning to a 15th century lifestyle, as I've been accused of promoting. If it is to become a mass movement that will help reduce the human impact on natural systems while providing opportunities for self-discovery and the development of talents valued by others, it will be necessary to have a better understanding of what all is encompassed by the phrase "cultural commons."

But first it is important to understand why staying within the dominant consumer-dependent and technologically oriented culture will not overcome the built-in limitations of a politics of scarcity. The politics of scarcity is now expressed in as many ways as scarcity exists—with a small group of the elite and super-rich possessing the power (i) to shape governmental decisions in ways that continue to benefit themselves economically, and (ii) to impose their ideology on the rest of society. For them, there is no scarcity in their ability to exercise political power. However, scarcity is very real for the underpaid, unemployed, and socially marginalized, and this scarcity translates into a lack of political power. Scarcity also exists for most public school graduates and for too many university graduates. It takes the form of lacking knowledge of the lifestyle changes needed to reduce the likelihood of their grandchildren facing social chaos as natural systems begin to fail. If this appears excessively alarmist, doing the math on when major systems are predicted to break down—such as aquifers (due to drought), oceans (due to acidification), climate (due to the global rise in temperatures), agriculture (due to loss of topsoil) — suggests that, if anything, the threat is understated.

As droughts continue, food costs rise for the already poor, and workers are displaced by computer systems, the politics of protest will move beyond the old tactic of street demonstrations. The different languages of persuasion have proven politically ineffective, as witnessed over the years by how environmental activism has failed to educate the public about the dangers of degrading the environment. And now, in the wake of Pope Francis' encyclical, Republicans and their billionaire supportors demonstrate what is more important to them by amassing material wealth and political power rather than addressing the deep cultural changes that must be undertaken in the immediate decades ahead. Items central to a market liberal agenda — the widely held myth of unending progress, a human-centered world, and the libertarian interpretation of individual autonomy — ensure that the environmental reforms of the Nixon presidency will not be repeated.

The Republicans and K Street lobbyists who are selling out the country's increasingly limited prospects for an ecologically sustainable future are working to reverse the environmental legislation of the Nixon era. They accomplish this by doing the bidding of the Chamber of Commerce, the corporations, and the billionaire free-market advocates. What remains of democratic decision-making is now directly under attack from a coalition of ideological, economic, and technological forces. This can be seen in (i) how state legislatures are now prohibiting local communities from passing laws that limit oil and gas exploration, (ii) efforts to limit the vote, (iii) how some states prohibit their employees from using words that refer to climate change, and (iv) the way the digital revolution has now bypassed democratic decision-making.

THE SLIPPERY SLOPE WE ARE NOW ON

Escaping the "downward spiral" in the political process may be the wrong metaphor to use, as what is really being proposed here is the recovery of local democracy. Local democracies can exist only in face-to-face communities where people understand the issues related to (i) improving the community's quality of life, and (ii) adopting practices that do not further degrade the self-renewing capacity of natural systems. There is a different kind of accountability in face-to-face communication, one that is grounded in moral values shaped by shared experiences and awareness that misrepresentation, exploitation, or acts of selfishness will only lead to distrust and affect future relationships.

What we now experience at the state and federal levels in the United States is a democracy in name only, as most decisions are the outcome of power relationships between key decision-makers. Corporate wealth is used to shape consciousness with politically coded images and slogans, reported in print, that provide only surface knowledge of the economic and ideological forces operating out of public view. All of this is overseen by a system of state and federal courts where a judges' ideology too often leads to decisions far removed from any form of face-to-face accountability or commitment to local democracy.

Of the many ideologically driven recent Supreme Court decisions that have undermined the democratic process, the Citizens United vs. Federal Election Commission decision is perhaps the most damaging, as those who wrote the majority opinion argued that the First Amendment to the Constitution prohibits government from regulating campaign spending by organizations such as for-profit corporations, trade unions, and so forth. In effect, this decision argued that corporations have the same free speech rights as individuals and that campaign donations are a form of free speech. Just as free speech cannot be limited, the amount of campaign donations cannot be limited. This has opened the floodgates to billionaires, such as the Koch brothers, who are changing the outcomes of state and federal elections by donating millions of dollars for candidates who share their libertarian/market liberal and anti-environment ideology.

Another example of how the current political system works against the interests of the average citizen by supporting the agenda of corporations can be seen in how Congress prohibited Medicare from negotiating the price of drugs with the pharmaceutical industry, as is done in Australia, Canada, and most European countries. With some drugs designed for cancer treatment now costing as much as a $150,000 a year, increasing numbers of patients are facing bankruptcy in their effort to extend life by a few months. In countries where the national medical system is allowed to negotiate prices, the cost of similar drugs varies from 40 to 70 percent less. That the current majority in Congress has no interest other than protecting the profits of corporations and the already super-rich can be seen in the fact that the 1000-page legislation prohibiting negotiation of lower drug prices was written by representatives of the pharmaceutical industry.

Computer scientists, working hand in hand with corporations and a public mesmerized by the convenience of seemingly unlimited access to information, are all greasing the slippery slope the nation is now on. We must keep in mind the Janus nature of digital technologies, just as we keep in mind the Janus nature of print and data. But the effort to digitize every aspect of human experience, and thus to create machines that surpass the uneven abilities of humans, is introducing changes not understood either by computer scientists or the public. The latter willingly fly the flag of progress with the same enthusiasm as the smiling citizens of Nazi Germany, who waved the swastika and believed the combination of mythic thinking and new technologies would bring about a more promising future.

We are on a similar slippery slope, but unlike the defeat of the Nazis and the restoration of German democracy, cultural changes resulting from the digital revolution cannot be reversed. This is partly because digital technologies have led to new knowledge in a variety of fields and to an increased dependence on technologies in all areas of life. They have become so integrated into daily life that few remember how tasks were carried out before the introduction of computers. There is no question the digital revolution has changed many aspects of life for the better. However, when we consider the other direction in which the Janus god faces, we have to ask if the increased efficiency, convenience, amazing advances in scientific knowledge, and technological breakthroughs have been overshadowed by what is being lost. We need to ask whether the social chaos arising from changes in the natural systems will lead to a data-driven form of fascism. Indeed, we may be so far down that slippery slope that social chaos will only be averted by scientists who will use the new nano-technologies and gene-editing technologies to alter consciousness and behaviors potentially disruptive of a world organized and controlled by super computers that are no longer under the control of human intelligence.

Before explaining how participating in the local cultural commons represents a less environmentally destructive lifestyle, as well as a way to escape from a future engineered by computer scientists and corporations still focused on the myth of unending progress, it is important to identify the irreversible changes spreading throughout the world, and that are now being accepted as the latest expression of progress.

MAKING CRAFT KNOWLEDGE AND PEOPLE REDUNDANT

The Industrial Revolution changed the community-centered craft guild systems of the medieval era in ways that reduced the worker to a wage earner performing repetitive tasks required by the design of the machine. It also disrupted the rhyme of the community as well as its patterns of mutual support. The digital and global phase of the Industrial Revolution is now making not only the skills but the workers themselves redundant. That is, robots are replacing workers on the assembly line and on the factory floor, while algorithms are replacing white collar jobs. The goal of computer scientists is to increase the autonomy of these computer systems to the point where their ability to retrieve vast amounts of data enables them to first define the problem, then set in motion computer solutions to the problem—all without human involvement. The immediate goal is driverless cars, trucks, airplanes—including commercial planes—military robots, kitchen appliances, and even robots that not only entertain but also function as helpful companions. With traditional jobs and careers becoming more limited, new fields beckon that are both intellectually stimulating and potential sources of vast wealth. I refer to the creation of new application software (apps) to replace the need for human reliance upon our own knowledge and skills. Already, more than 30 percent of the American workforce is limited to contingency work in what is also being referred to as the "sharing" economy. This development is being represented as showing the increasing entrepreneurial spirit of the American worker, but the reality is that in a "sharing" economy there is no minimum wage, no retirement or health benefits, and no worker safety provisions, all of which could be had in the old system of full-time employment.

At least two factors are driving the adoption of robotic and algorithmic systems, both of which further displace workers: (i) the environmental crisis is leading to more focus on increasing the efficiency of existing technologies, and, (ii) the growing pressure of globalization is giving an economic advantage to countries with lower wages and lower environmental standards. What is happening in the Pearl River Delta of China is a case in point. The new growth market in this region is the manufacture of industrial robots, with 1,500 being produced last year. For China as a whole, sales of robotic technologies reached 5.6 million units. The number of workers made redundant by robots varies depending upon the production process, but at the Guangdong Everwin Precision Technology Company, the introduction of 60 industrial robots reduced the number of needed workers by 600. This global trend is an indication of how progress will be understood and measured in the future.

The robotics trend is being repeated in other parts of the world along with the myth that replacement of workers by robots will lead to technologies that create new jobs. This myth exemplifies a deliberate social deception on the part of computer scientists and corporate promoters of the digital revolution. It conceals some key questions: (i) how will an increasing percentage of the world's population make a living, while the owners of technologies become increasingly wealthy, and (ii) how will society change, given that robots do not contribute to the social security system or pay the taxes essential to sustaining a society's' infrastructure? At some point, more people will recognize that they are caught in a cycle where the drive to replace humans with machines will reduce their incomes, which will slow the pace of consumerism, which in turn will lead corporations to reduce labor costs by—again—replacing employees with automated systems. Thus, the cycle of increased unemployment will accelerate.

That increasingly autonomous technologies will not lead to new career paths should be obvious, but there has not been a serious national debate about whether the vision of progress held by computer scientists and their corporate supporters is viable. As I have made clear, computer scientists, as well as the libertarian/market liberal ideologues who guide corporate decisions, do not have a deep understanding of the cultures into which their technologies are being introduced. Slogans about unending progress continue to reassure the public. But slogans about the inevitability of progress are abstractions that will not put food on the table and will not save us from our misuse of the environment. At some point an inability to participate in the money economy, due to its takeover by computers, will lead people to move from their current state of embracing the digital revolution to violent protests.

WHO BENEFITS FROM THE LOSS OF PRIVACY AND SECURITY?

Unlike the question of how to change consciousness on a sufficiently massive scale that people begin to exercise ecological intelligence, the question of who benefits from the loss of personal privacy and security is easy to answer. The winners in this increasingly Social Darwinian world are the computer scientists, corporations, and government agencies monitoring the ideas and behaviors of citizens; hackers who steal people's identities; and foreign governments and corporations that are able to spy on technological advances and governmental operations. Compared to what is being lost, what the average citizen gains beyond convenience and increased efficiency in performing different task is an increasingly a moot question.

The argument made by many people, including Mark Zuckerberg, is that people who live law-abiding lives will not experience constant electronic surveillance of their every activity as a threat to their civil liberties. Surveillance, according to this way of thinking, deters people who may engage in unlawful activities. But expanding electronic surveillance of people's behaviors, beyond even the East German Stasi, undermines a democratic society. Just consider: future debates may become so heated that those who control the police may use their surveillance technologies to suppress any questioning of their economic agendas. The FBI's surveillance of Martin Luther King, Jr., on the fabricated charge of his communist leanings, serves as a warning of how the NSA, the FBI, and other policing agencies within the government are subject to being controlled by the very groups whose activities are being challenged.

As basic natural resources become more limited, as weather becomes more extreme, and as unemployment increases, tensions are likely to rise. This will lead to political activism that replicates the anti-war protests of the 60's and 70's. Governmental agencies, which are controlled by the ideologies of politicians and bureaucrats, will not be neutral. Access to data, including the use of new technologies—such as facial recognition systems connected to massive databanks—will move us further down the slippery slope to being a police state.

Surveillance systems will be more omnipresent as the estimated 25–30 billion "smart" devices and objects (now referred to as the Internet of Things, or the Internet of Everything) monitor changes in our bodies, activities in our households, and our interactions with others. Everything from toasters to house lighting systems will have built-in sensors. Our clothes ("wearable computing") will have wireless connectivity to the Internet. Thus doctors, pharmaceutical companies, employers (and future employers), companies wishing to push their products, teachers/professors, security agencies, utility providers, and computer-savvy neighbors will have access to the data collected on every aspect of our lives and stored in the cloud. There will be benefits, such as being able to turn on smart coffee machines, water plants showing signs of distress, obtain information on the Dionysian lifestyle of a future employee, learn who was in bed in the early afternoon and with whom, and send changes in our physical condition that enable doctors to give medical advice by email or Skype.

But did we vote on surrendering our lives to this level of surveillance? Can we believe the experts, given their past record of failure, that the data will be protected by totally reliable security systems? Has the indifference of our classroom teachers to the importance of serious discussions about the non-neutrality of technologies, especially digital technologies, contributed to undermining what remains of our democracy (not already subverted by corporate and elite interests)?

As noted earlier, *The Future of Violence: Robots and Germs, Hackers and Drones—Confronting a New Age of Threat*, by Benjamin Wittes and Gabriella Blum, needs to be read by everyone—including those who deny that there is an ecological crisis. The authors document what is being ignored as computer scientists, corporations, classroom teachers, and professors—flying the banner of unending progress—promote the expansion of digital culture without giving serious consideration to the dangers that lie ahead or the cultural traditions being lost. While the Internet and the ability to digitize knowledge and wealth are beneficial in many ways, the vulnerabilities they create are not widely understood. Indeed, the effort to promote coding in the early grades, as is occurring in England and other Western counties, is an example of how the myth of technologically driven progress makes all other considerations irrelevant.

It is unfortunate that the warnings of Wittes and Blum were not heard before computer scientists started down the path of global connectivity, and that they did not heed the warnings of earlier generations of scientists about the dangers of making certain forms of technical knowledge, such as how to build atomic bombs, available to everyone. Instead of creating a Union of Concerned Computer Scientists, we have computer scientists promoting their technology in the same missionary manner as Christian fundamentalists who were driven to save the world by converting it to their image. Typical of this lack of caution is Eric Schmidt and Jared Cohen's book, *The New Digital Age: Reshaping the Future of People, Nations, and Business* (2103). They even make the naïve argument that access to data will ensure that democratic decision-making will prevail over any misuse of digital technologies. But it is the message in *The Future of Violence* that is proving to be the more accurate account of what has emerged from the Pandora's box that has now been opened. As Wittes and Blum write:

> To put it bluntly, we are all in the same boat now, one in which we are vulnerable to surveillance, theft, harassment, and even physical attacks from a variety of actors capable of pursuing us with diminished accountability for their actions.... This raises another feature of the new vulnerability: it knows no

geographical boundaries. Just as you cannot hide behind the lock on your front door, national borders do not offer an effective barrier against the spread of viruses, whether biological or electronic, or against information exploitation or remotely operated weapons. (57)

To make the point more succinctly, everyone is now vulnerable to any person or group anywhere in the world who possesses the technological knowledge to hack into systems and engage in cyberattacks on utilities and other governmental infrastructures. The state, as the authors point out, is no longer able to protect us from those near and abroad who want to disrupt our lives.

There are other losses that largely go unnoticed by the proponents of digitizing more aspects of daily life. These include the change in consciousness that comes with spending many hours of the day glued to a computer screen that provides instantaneous access to the abstractions encoded in the printed word, data, and visual images. Educators have celebrated computer-mediated learning as enabling students to construct their own understandings and values. Lost are the narratives passed forward in face-to-face communication that provide an awareness of how the present reproduces the wisdom, misconceptions, and silences of the past. These narratives are often examples of unexamined myths and prejudices that should not have been enacted in the first place, but they also include the struggles for greater social justice. Having access to data and the ability to communicate with anyone anywhere has led to many benefits, but this connectivity in the abstract world of the Internet has also enabled people with hateful agendas to find support from others who also want to remain hidden.

THE CULTURAL COMMONS IN AN INCREASINGLY DANGEROUS WORLD

Cultural alternatives to the individually centered industrial/consumer-dependent lifestyle (now recognized as a major contributor to climate change) continue to exist in every community and in every culture. Indeed, they have existed since the first humans shared knowledge of where to obtain food, how to prepare it, how to bury their dead, how to develop technologies, and how to use them. That is, the knowledge, skills, and mentoring that were not monetized and thus shared intergenerationally among the first humans have been carried forward in culture-guiding mythopoetic narratives. These stories have been continually revised to fit the diversity of environmental challenges and changes in each culture.

Regardless of social status and level of formal education, everyone today relies upon the cultural commons of their family, ethnic group, and the larger shared culture. These intergenerational traditions of knowledge and skill are largely taken for granted and thus not recognized as an alternative form of wealth that exists outside the money economy. Increasingly, they are being recognized as community-centered lifestyle alternatives that (i) have a smaller ecological footprint, and (ii) represent approaches to work where the individual's craft knowledge and skill lead to creating what is useful to the community rather than being driven by machine technologies to produce for the mass market. The cultural commons are recognized as absolutely essential in many cultures around the world. They continue to carry forward, in the face of the West's colonizing pressures, traditions responsive to the uniqueness of their bioregions and guiding mythopoetic narratives.

If our educational systems, media, and elites such as philosophers, social theorists, and even liberal arts graduates had depended less on technologies that promote abstract thinking and more on a balanced approach to learning that includes cultural awareness, there might be wider recognition of the importance of the cultural commons. The cultural commons, which everyone relies upon but largely takes for granted, includes shared language, recipes for preparing and preserving food, narratives, different creative arts, and linguistic patterns that govern patterns of meta-communication. We even rely upon those aspects of the cultural commons that reproduce the prejudices and misconceptions of earlier generations — in the same way English speakers take for granted the subject/verb/object pattern of organizing and expressing their thoughts. And these thoughts largely reproduce the metaphorical patterns of thinking of earlier generations!

The point to be emphasized here is that the taken-for-granted cultural commons need to be made explicit and critically understood as alternatives to the dominant culture—a culture now driven by techno-utopians whose proposals would (i) replace humans with machines in the workplace, (ii) promote non-democratic decision-making, and (iii) reduce human lives to data that will be exploited by corporations, hackers, and surveillance-addicted governments.

Perhaps if the educational system had not relegated face-to-face and largely non-monetized intergenerational forms of knowledge and skills carried on in every community to such a lower status, then people would be able to acknowledge that expansion of the industrial/consumer approach to progress will only accelerate further destruction of the environment. Awareness of climate change without any sense of the existing cultural alternatives leaves us in the same confused state of powerlessness as our leading politicians who are in denial about the relationship between consumer-dependent industrial culture and environmental degradation.

Giving close attention to the otherwise taken-for-granted cultural ways of thinking and behavioral patterns, which are also part of the more broadly shared cultural commons, brings into focus other intergenerational traditions that need to be carried forward. These include such gains in social justice as forcing King John to sign the Magna Carta; or passing legislation to (i) prohibit the exploitation of child labor, (ii) enable women to vote and to escape previous cultural restrictions, (iii) allow for some environmental protections, and so forth. All of these social justice gains resulted when people became, so to speak, their own ethnographers. They paid attention to where and how they were being restricted by older prejudices; where and how they were being exploited by economic and political interests outside their own.

A "perfect storm" of destructive forces is coming together: (i) chemical changes in the world's oceans, (ii) rising temperatures, (iii) loss of species and habitats, (iv) increasing numbers of people facing food and water shortages, (v) the digitizing and globalization of industrial culture, with an accompanying loss of local knowledge and skills, (vi) the increasing displacement of people by digital technologies, (vii) impending perpetual armed struggle against colonization and increasingly scarce resources, (viii) greater connectivity reducing every aspect of daily life to data, and (ix) increasing control of the political process by ideologues and the super-rich. In the face of all this, it is critically important to acknowledge resistance: people worldwide are recovering the importance of the cultural commons—and are finding ways to participate.

Unfortunately, these people represent only a small minority within Western cultures, and many indigenous cultures still struggle to renew their cultural commons intergenerationally, as their youth are seduced by the commercialism and digital technologies of the West. Whether the diversity of the world's cultural commons will survive beyond the end of this century is problematic, but they represent the best hope. They also represent community zones of safety from the surveillance technologies of hackers, corporations, and governments. Face-to-face relationships, local barter and mutual exchange economies, and face-to-face decision-making about the needs of the community (i.e., local democracy) do not leave an electronic footprint that can be turned into the data profiles now used to invade peoples' privacy.

Why use the phrase "cultural commons" rather than "community"? The main reason is that the word "community" is too general. It is too open to interpretations that lack a key part of the vocabulary associated with the phrase "cultural commons." What the commonplace use of the word "community" lacks is the special sense given to the cultural commons by another word, namely, "enclosure." That is, the concept of the cultural commons includes the possible threat of enclosure, which is the process by which something that is shared in common is turned into something privately owned, then monetized and integrated into the industrial/market economy.

The vocabulary of the cultural commons is associated with the enclosure movement that swept through England during the Industrial Revolution, a time when the move to ownership of common lands benefited wealthy landowners at the expense of those who previously had free use of common areas for crops or grazing. Thus today's use of the phrase "cultural commons" has often been misinterpreted as an appeal to return to the pre-industrial lifestyle of earlier centuries. This misconception would not exist if people were explicitly aware of the cultural commons carried forward in their families, communities, and even within the dominant culture.

One hopes this awareness would also enable them to recognize how various economic and technological agendas, ranging from greater reliance upon digital technologies to (i) educational reforms such as the Common Core Curriculum, (ii) the appeal for engaging more students in a liberal education, and (iii) the growing spread of conservative (market liberal) thinking, are contributing to the further enclosure of the cultural commons. The skills and knowledge that were passed forward intergenerationally enabled people to become more self-reliant outside of the industrial system of production and consumption. These skills are now being undermined by the flood of images carefully crafted to show how consumer products will improve quality of life. Knowledge becomes privatized and is integrated into the market economy, making people more dependent upon the money economy—an economy that is now being transformed by the digital revolution. The need for workers will become increasingly limited to those who possess the highly specialized knowledge required for participating in the digitized systems of production and services. In effect, a smaller number of people will have high salaries while the larger number of people will face increasing levels of economic insecurity.

Given that Common Core curriculum reforms were heavily promoted by corporate interests and thus emphasized preparing students for problem solving in increasingly automated work settings, the students caught in this educationally driven pyramid scheme of false promises will be left without a knowledge of the alternative sources of wealth and mutual support that are part of a cultural commons-centered life.

Print-based learning, earlier ways of thinking encoded in metaphorical language, as well as the silences, contribute to ignoring the importance of what is taken for granted in the patterns of everyday life. But it is impossible to entirely ignore these patterns, especially when the contradictions and false promises begin to impact daily life more directly—which is happening today as marginalized groups protest against barriers they now recognize more clearly.

The argument being made here, which is supportive of, yet largely ignored by, these liberation efforts, is that a pathway to a less environmentally and humanly destructive life exists. It can be recognized in the daily practices and mutually supportive relationships that are less monetized and that reduce the need for a consumerism that is contributing to an ecological crisis that will shortly overwhelm all other issues. In addition to becoming liberated from the institutionalized prejudices of earlier eras, there is an equally important need to discover personal talents and interests, to achieve a deeper level of self-discovery and competence by learning from achievements of the past in the arts, crafts, social justice, and wisdom traditions, none of which can be met by more consumerism.

Contrary to the misconception that an individual's freedom is more fully expressed when she/he engages in creative activities supposedly free of all historical influences, the reality is that the mastery of a *tradition*—in the arts, working with wood or stone, preparing a special meal and sharing it with others—is essential to self-discovery and self-realization. But it is the expression of a personal freedom that is situated in a larger cultural ecology, here named as the cultural commons. That is, like face-to-face communication, self-discovery is part of the process of developing skills and talents that build on the non-commoditized traditions of the cultural commons and that will, in turn, become the basis of self-discovery and self-expression of future generations.

What are examples of cultural commons activities and support systems in cities, in suburbia, in rural areas? What is distinctive about different ethnic cultural commons—their approaches to the sharing of food, healing practices, narratives, ceremonies, creative arts, craft skills and knowledge, games, patterns of mentoring and mutual support, approachs to social justice issues, their ecology of language and identity, and the mentors who will engage youth in the existential processes of self-discovery? There is a need to map within different communities the cultural commons activities, as well as to identify mentors in how to find fulfillment in more community-centered lives. Within each area of the cultural commons there are wisdom keepers who understand the wealth shared within the cultural commons and the spiritual poverty of those who extract other people's potential by reducing them to consumers and making them replaceable by machines.

There is also a need to make explicit how the cultural commons are being enclosed. People are born into a world saturated with commercials, with an overwhelming number of choices, with constant promises of how buying goods and services extolled by beautiful experts will add to even more happiness and success. All of this is so taken for granted that public spaces *not* exploited by the sounds and images of commercial culture become the oddities. We assume that assaults on consciousness and self-identity are a normal part of daily life. If this is all one knows, it will feel more like home and less demanding.

Ethnographic mapping needs to be done to show how different technologies may be empowering, but also work together to undermine the very existence of the cultural commons. As noted earlier, an overreliance upon print-based cultural storage and thinking promotes the Western cultural bias toward abstraction, which fosters the illusion that rational, even critical thought is supposedly free of cultural influences. This reinforces the misconception that an individual has a unique, unmediated experience of the world, and that giving close attention to cultural patterns that connect is irrelevant.

An overreliance upon print-based communication makes it appear unnecessary to take oral traditions seriously — especially when they are being passed forward by older people whose ideas are now viewed as outdated. A similar pattern exists in relation to data; that is, we rely on data without taking seriously that it begins with culturally influenced decisions about what behaviors are to be the source of the data, and that it is interpreted by a culturally influenced way of thinking (hidden by references to data interpreters as "data scientists"). In both instances, this overreliance is an impediment to the face-to-face, contextual, intergenerational communication that is essential to the renewal of the cultural commons.

If we consider the patterns of apprenticeship in the guild systems of the medieval era, as well as the control workers exercised before Taylorism led to the scientific study of how to maximize both efficiency and profits in the workplace (and now to replace the worker entirely with digital machines), we can see major obstacles to carrying forward the craft knowledge and skill that were part of the heritage of different cultural commons. Techniques and technologies that are now the dominant feature of modern life are eliminating a wide range of cultural commons knowledge and skills as the older generation dies off. In place of this face-to-face sharing, which was also about moral development and learning to be cautious, there is now application software that dispenses with the development of character by providing expert, culture-free knowledge about how to carry out most tasks in life. These apps become, like other aspects of the digital culture that are seeping into every nook and cranny of life, an inescapable and indispensable tool of the surveillance technologies that are constantly gathering and sharing our private data—which turns us into objects for others to watch for vulnerabilities that can be exploited.

One political consequence of the Western myth of the autonomous individual is that it supports another cultural construction, namely, that property can be privately owned—and that personal success is achieved by owning as much as possible. The patenting of ideas and creative works, as well as the ownership of land, are largely taken for granted in the West, although there is a small movement recognizing that creative works are the outcome of sharing and informal cultural influences on the individual who integrates these into a slightly original form. It is important to note that these achievements are made part of the "creative commons" and are freely available.

The larger issue here is how the mutually supportive ideas of individualism and private ownership continually contribute to the enclosure of the cultural commons. These ideas are not universals, as is supposed, but part of the cultural inheritance of Western philosophers and social theorists who were unaware that these ideas are not shared in many of the world's cultural commons. The emphasis on private ownership has led to the reach of corporate culture into the ideas and practices of individuals and communities in order to expand their product lines and increase profits. It does not matter to these on-steroids entrepreneurial individuals and corporations that to privatize and then monetize skills and knowledge that previously were part of the cultural commons increases dependence upon a money economy that has become increasingly unfair. Nor do they recognize the catastrophic consequences of turning what was intergenerationally passed forward into an industrially produced product with a larger ecological footprint.

Ecologically sustainable cultural patterns do exist and are modeled in many families and communities. But the over emphasis on abstract thinking that results from privileging print as a higher form of knowledge has marginalized these patterns. There is a close connection between this kind of marginalization and the above forms of enclosure, because the cultural commons heritage is a daily source of empowerment, and when attention is no longer paid, this vital resource is lost.

The failure to do the ethnographic work of making these patterns explicit is compounded by the failure of classroom teachers and university professors to provide the language and theory frameworks that would enable students to recognize aspects of their taken-for-granted worlds that are sources of empowerment and community. When classroom teachers and professors *do* bring cultural commons practices into focus, it is usually to help students recognize patterns of discrimination and exploitation, of which there are many. This is vitally important, but it is generally framed in terms of an ideology that reinforces the idea that the primary purpose of critical thinking is to overturn all traditions that stand in the way of achieving social justice and thus progress. This ideology does not consider critical attention to ideas that would reduce our dependence upon a money economy and have a smaller adverse ecological impact, nor does it consider the cultural commons as a source of skills and supporting relationships.

What the myth of progress has done is to turn critical thinking into a process of emancipation from *all* traditions, with little understanding that many traditions were formed when survival depended upon communities of mutual support and self-reliance, and that these traditions now represent sites of resistance to an industrial/consumer-dependent life. If critical inquiry were to be more balanced, the focus would also be on what needs to be conserved. And this would lead to examining how print, data, robots, culturally uninformed computer scientists, and market liberal ideologies, along with mythic thinking about the autonomous individual, private property, free markets, and the other historically rogue cultural patterns contribute to the enclosure of the cultural commons.

≈ 8 ≈

Educational Reforms that Revitalize the
Cultural Commons

A PARADIGM SHIFT WILL BE REQUIRED if today's children, when they reach the mid- to late decades of the 21st century, will not be engulfed in a world of deprivation, social conflict over increasingly scarce resources, the merging of total surveillance technologies within a police state, and tactics that include the use of consciousness-changing drugs. Making the transition to this new paradigm will actually be a matter of recovering key characteristics of community-centered lives—that which represented the mainstream of human history before the Industrial Revolution, with its myth of progress and abstract justifications for placing profits and environmental exploitation above all other values. Many of the intergenerational skills and knowledge inherited from these pre-industrial local cultures continue to be part of today's taken-for-granted world, like seeds waiting for the right combination of social conditions to grow.

In addition to the cultural commons practices carried forward in these forms of empowerment, such as knowing how to grow and preserve vegetables, there are other examples of face-to-face interactions that strengthen community and represent multiple forms of economic interdependence. These include the use of local currencies and barter practices, the local farmer's markets that are expanding around the country, and the many ways in which local businesses and even banks are supporting the spreading localism movement. For examples, the Business Alliance for Local Living Economies (BALLE) is actively promoting businesses that support local communities in all phases of production across the United States and Canada, as well as working with other groups committed to the localism model as an alternative to the global industrial/consumer model of development. Other groups committed to this paradigm shift include the Schumacher Center for New Economics, Helena Norberg-Hodge's Local Futures/International Society for Ecology and Culture, the transition communities spreading across southern England and being adopted in other regions of the world, the Slow Food Movement, the Land Institute, and the Indigenous and First Nations movements spread across the Americas. The efforts of Indigenous cultures in other parts of the world to intergeneration-ally renew their cultural commons traditions must also be noted. The localism movement exists in nearly every community and focuses on (i) growing food without the use of harmful chemicals and pesticide, (ii) promoting locally made goods and services that rely upon recovery of the bartering practices of pre-industrial cultures, and (iii) reducing dependency upon the fossil fuel/industrial culture that survives only by degrading the Earth's natural systems.

Those in the localism movement rely on modern science and tech-nologies, but their use is guided by an ideology that makes mutually supportive local communities, rather than profits, the primary focus. This revival of localism is also based on face-to-face democracy. Other virtues, that should be more widely understood as the world becomes increasingly stressed by environmental disruptions and climate-in-duced migrations, are that face-to-face communities are a refuge from the industrial culture's obsession with reducing life processes to data, from experts who earn their living by creating psychological and social problems that only they can fix, and from robots and other computer systems designed to replace humans. In short, the diversity of localism movements, with all their cultural forms of expression, represents a way to recover the best expressions of our humanity and a spiritual sense of connectedness within the layered cultural and nature ecologies of which we are an integral part.

This brief overview is intended to remind anyone thinking about educational reforms that there are a wealth of cultural commons-oriented groups that exist under a variety of labels. If we begin to think about where and how to start introducing students to survival pathways that help them avoid the growing scarcities—ranging from jobs, to natural resources, to sources of wisdom in this age of scientism and techno-utopian thinking—then educational reforms must begin with local cultural practices. This means the starting point will involve making explicit the interconnections between language and taken-for-granted beliefs and practices.

Reading about the cultural commons will provide an initial vocabulary for developing explicit awareness of what would otherwise be the largely presupposed cultural patterns handed down within the family, ethnic communities, and the larger society. But like so much of what is read, it is likely to remain yet another encounter with an external and thus abstract world. Reading, for all its benefits, will not put the student on the long pathway to self-discovery that comes from prolonged engagement in one of the arts, working with some form of material culture, or acquiring the intergenerational knowledge of the bioregion. Self-discovery, contrary to today's thinking, is more than a flash-in-the-pan excitement of doing something for the first time. Rather, it involves (i) the coming together of an ecologically informed interpretive framework (more about this later), (ii) a prolonged physical/mental encounter with some aspect of the material and symbolic culture, and (iii) mentors to play the role of the mediator who helps clarify dimensions of the experience that would otherwise go unrecognized, such as the work of others who moved the achievements of the past to new levels.

But further clarification is needed before explaining how the above can be understood as a model for introducing students to the cultural commons and how this leads to a transformative experience. First, ecological intelligence, which was introduced earlier, needs further clarification. And, given the relational world in which we live, the exercise of ecological intelligence would be misunderstood if we retained the idea, reinforced by a print- and data-based culture, that we live in a world of fixed and enduring entities. Just as there are no straight lines in nature, there are no independent entities, including ideas and values, that are not influenced by the ongoing relationships and information exchanges occurring within the layered and interdependent natural and cultural ecologies. The rational process, when represented as being free of cultural (that is, linguistic) influence, cannot take full account of what is distinct about ecologies; namely, that everything in this world of diverse eco-semiotic patterns communicates. What Bateson refers to as the difference that makes a difference in the response of the Other, whether at the level of the smallest organism or among humans, is ongoing, and thus the source of continual changes in relationships. A reified understanding of progress, for example, remains unchallenged when it is used uncritically as a basis for judging different technologies. But when the idea of progress is framed within an emergent context wherein a technology is recognized as contributing to, say, the deskilling of workers or to birth deformities, then the idea becomes questionable. This then leads to the next question: "Who benefits from the harm being done to others?" The meaning of ideas, as in an ongoing conversation, changes as the idea is understood in terms of other relationships. Reified ideas, on the other hand, retain a fixed meaning along with the other abstractions.

Daily life, too, often involves reliance upon two levels of intelligence. The modern form of intelligence, which is heavily influenced by an overreliance on learning from printed accounts (which are inherently abstract) and by unquestioned assumptions about the autonomous individual, is constantly reinforced at so many levels of communication. Communiucation occurs with others through the media and other technologies, and through curricula that prepares students for work in this dominant economic and technological culture, where things and even relationships are monetized.

But as we live in emergent, relational, cultural, and natural ecologies, involving networks of constant communication, it is impossible to escape exercising ecological intelligences. The impermanence of life leads to constant awareness—or at least it should. Unfortunately, overreliance on the abstract world, derived in part from print-based cultural storage and communication, has left the mind filled with abstract ideas, values, and interpretative frameworks that are assumed to be unchanging. This is the mythic world that leads to the certainty of individual intelligence. The difference between individual and even the individually centered exercise of ecological intelligence is similar to the difference Martin Buber recognized between the I-It relationships of monologues and the I-Thou relationships that come into play with dialogue. Dialogue, like the exercise of ecological intelligence, involves responding to the ongoing flow of multiple levels of information exchange in (i) conversing with another person, (ii) giving attention to the complex and rapidly changing messages being communicated at a busy intersection, (ii) recognizing where, in a musical performance, one is to enter the flow of the performance, (iii) recognizing and responding on the playing field to the behavior of an opponent, and so forth. In effect, the exercise of ecological intelligence is an essential and inescapable aspect of negotiating one's way through both the most routine as well as special situations where changes (that is, where differences make a difference) are constant.

What is not adequately recognized is how the deep assumptions of a culture influence the exercise of ecological intelligence. The language learned from others too often hides the taken-for-granted cultural patterns — including how the myth of individuality leads to being self-centered. Individually centered awareness of the multiple and interactive communication networks that are part of any natural or cultural context — such as walking in the forest or socializing at a gathering — involves a series of existential concerns. How am I going to say what needs to be said to this other person? How am I going to avoid the boring person walking toward me? How do I greet someone I haven't seen for years? That is, individually centered ecological intelligence is largely driven by pragmatic concerns: How to adapt one's behaviors in ways that take account of the local ecology — of messages and other people's behaviors — in ways that lead to achieving one's personal objectives.

Learning the language of one's culture may also lead to acquiring what earlier generations ignored, that is, the silences that provide formulaic explanations of how to think about such things as data, progress, traditions, success, and so forth. The power of a largely inherited language to carry forward the silences of previous generations can be seen in how the individually centered exercise of ecological intelligence has precluded considering the impact of one's decisions on the self-renewing capacity of natural systems. Consider the individually centered ecological intelligence exercised in a new car purchase: the salesperson, the intelligence behind the aesthetics of the showroom, as well as the design elements of the car all merge into multiple levels of communication. Too often ignored is the amount of carbon dioxide the car will put into the atmosphere. Most consumer decisions reflect this individually centered form of ecological intelligence, even though awareness of climate change is occurring. Consumers just don't think relationally, which is characteristic of overreliance on print, data, and English nouns.

In short, if the next generation is to escape the death spiral caused by the mythical ideas of the autonomous individual, a human-centered world, and progress, it will be necessary for educators at all levels of formal and informal education to adopt the role of a mediator who helps students clarify which of the cultural patterns, practices, ideas, and values that they daily engage will have a smaller, less destructive impact on the natural and cultural ecologies on which their futures depend. That is, to help students recognize the relational ecologies in which they live and on which they are absolutely dependent, it needs to become second nature to consider the impact of personal decisions on the health of both the natural and cultural ecologies. This awareness is not part of a person's DNA; it is learned from others who possess the wisdom that we live in an interconnected, emergent, and fragile world.

Moving beyond the individually centered exercise of ecological intelligence as well as leaving behind a life based on the abstractions of Western philosophers and social theorists involves a radically different approach than the liberal arts education proposed by Deresiewicz, as well as the Common Core curriculum, and from what characterizes most public school and university classrooms. It cannot be "delivered" by computers, and it cannot be machine tested. Rather, it involves educators who combine being mentors with being explicitly aware of how many of the cultural patterns reenacted in daily life contribute to lifestyles destructive to the environment and to the community.

Like the role of the mediator in a labor dispute, the teacher's role as a mediator requires deep understanding of the issues and unquestioned patterns that divide the two sides. That is, will a student's future life choices slow or accelerate the forces leading to the 6th great extinction? This is an important challenge facing educational reformers, who must escape from the misconceptions underlying the current understanding of progress.

The educator's role as that of a mediator is profoundly different from the two extremes that have dominated past thinking. One extreme framed the educator's role as introducing students to the ideas of important thinkers and engaging them in abstract debates that were both ethnocentric and totally dismissive of local cultural commons as sustainable alternatives to the emerging industrial culture. The other extreme, favored by so called progressive educators, involved reinforcing students in thinking they are morally and conceptually autonomous agents in a world where progress depends upon everyone continually searching for new ideas and values. The consequence of ignoring cultural ecologies as an inescapable part of life-giving and sustaining processes continues to influence both the present and future. It has led to the same surface, and thus mistake-ridden, misconceptions that characterize the thinking of computer scientists— who are now working, in the name of progress, to replace humans with machines.

THE PRACTICE OF CULTURAL COMMONS EDUCATION

The practice of a cultural commons-oriented pedagogy and curriculum involves relying upon cultural examples that open doors to a variety of interpretations. And because the conceptual framework being introduced here will be new to many readers, the cultural examples may lead to a variety of misunderstandings. Also, the way print undermines awareness of the importance of contexts, as well as the emergent and relational nature of what is being described, leads to generalizations that are in themselves easily misunderstood. To reduce misunderstandings, I suggest that readers adopt a more ethnographically informed assessment of my proposals. Hopefully, this will lead to recognition of the Janus (that is, both the constructive and destructive) nature of the cultural examples to which I refer, such as (i) when science is transformed into scientism, (ii) when print empowers or introduces a new status system, (iii) when computers serve socially useful purposes or the interests of elite groups, and (iv) when such concepts as individualism and progress contribute to social justice, and when they lead to the exploitation of others. Hopefully, readers will find examples in their own experience that corresponds to the examples used here that will help students become explicitly aware of their cultural commons experiences, as well as the forces of enclosure.

Printed material introduces an asymmetrical power relationship that obstructs the immediate exchange that would lead to greater clarification. So I ask readers to consider my examples and suggestions by relating them to their own ethnographically informed understanding of similar contexts and issues—not to dismiss them because they do not support the reader's abstract world of ideas and values. What is urgently needed, which I suggested in *Cultural Literacy for Freedom* (1974), is the ability to "read" (that is, make explicit) the otherwise taken-for-granted cultural patterns that are environmentally destructive. Who would have imagined the environment would change so rapidly in the 40-plus years since that book was published that scientists would be warning that we are entering the 6th extinction of life as we know it?

A PEDAGOGICAL MODEL OF MEDIATING
BETWEEN THE TWO CULTURES

The most important questions that educational reformers need to consider are (i) how to introduce students to the cultural pathways leading to a sustainable future and (ii) how to escape excessive commercialism and digital surveillance (with all its political and social consequences). The following examples show how the educator's mediating role leads to connecting the student's linguistic/conceptual development in ways that are grounded. This is achieved by making the student's taken-for-granted cultural patterns explicit and showing how they can serve as the model for learning not only about what is shared in common within the community, but also about the forces of enclosure.

Instead of reading about the cultural commons and the Janus nature of different technologies and beliefs, or listening to the conceptual educational orthodoxies that have brought us to this environmental tipping point, the educator should begin by introducing students to a comparative examination of cultural practices that characterize the cultural commons and techno/consumerism. As a mediator, the educator's role is not to provide an explanation of how students are to think about the advantages and disadvantages of each culture. Rather it is to provide examples from the consumer/industrial culture as well as corresponding examples from the cultural commons, and to ask the students to describe their different experiences in these two cultures. For example, the educator should ask students to describe first the consumer experience of buying food in a supermarket and then the experience within a family of growing and sharing their own food. Or it could be the experiential differences in watching and listening to the performances of others or engaging in learning the skills necessary for one's own performance. Or the differences between, on the one hand, a work setting where the task has been broken into segments that require rapid action and focused attention to repeat the same physical and conception pattern, or, on the other hand, engaging in a project that involves not only the conceptualization—including an assessment of the product's social usefulness and environmental impact—but also the skills and conceptual involvement reequired at every step in order to complete the project.

The educator's mediating role involves giving the student the conceptual space necessary for putting into words or art (that is, making explicit) the full range of differences in cultural patterns and relationships. This may include awareness of whether the salesperson communicates genuine interest in the student as a person or as simply a customer wherein the verbal exchange is formulaic. There are other life-shaping differences in the two cultures, such as which ones lead to the discovery of an interest that previously undiscovered, as well as the development of a skill and interest that comes from one's own sustained practice. Which of the two cultures is likely to lead to mentoring relationships and to becoming bonded in ways that create a sense of community? There will be times when the preconceptions learned from earlier moments of primary socialization will have led to the acceptance of others' thinking as so natural that it prevents the student from recognizing the fundamental differences between the two cultures. There will be times when this prior learning will lead to a formulaic rejection of ideas from the cultural commons that present an alternative to non-monetized forms of wealth that are not dependent upon destroying the environment.

The mediating role may require posing questions and even providing students with a vocabulary that enables them to articulate what was not previously possible, given the limited vocabulary acquired from others. By creating the conceptual space necessary for students to sort out the existential and empowering differences between cultural commons and industrial/consumer-dependent experiences, it is more likely that students will recognize the importance of participating more fully in the community's cultural commons. While there are important sources of empowerment in the industrial/scientific/technologically based mainstream culture, students are more likely to be aware of the disempowering and environmentally destructive side. That is, they are more likely to avoid accepting technological and market innovations on the basis that they are necessary to social progress. In addition to becoming explicitly aware of their taken-for-granted world, students will also be developing the conceptual and linguistic basis for exercising the communicative competence necessary for democratic decision-making—which is a necessary part of the cultural commons experience.

As students learn to give close attention to the multiple differences between their experience in cultural commons activities and their experience as consumers and in work settings increasingly subordinated to the dictates of machines, they also need to be introduced to the range of cultural commons activities carried on within the community. That is, the curriculum needs to be expanded by having students engage in a cultural survey of the individuals and networks that support such cultural commons activities as the local theater, musicians, dance, visual artists, writers, weavers, ceramic potters, wood carvers and metalworkers, organic farmers, people engaged in habitat restoration—as well as the skilled and professional people who participate in the local exchange economy.

Face-to-face conversations with those who sustain the wealth of the cultural commons can lead to learning about how each of these activities is part of a larger support network, and how these networks are part of the local exchange and barter economy. They can also lead to learning who the mentors are and how being a mentor adds to the quality of life—which is also part of the process of self-discovery. How much money does one need to live well in these networks of mutual support? Does involvement in cultural commons activities lead to reducing what has become an addiction in the mainstream culture to buying the latest fashion and digital technology? The answers to these questions will be especially useful to students concerned with how digital technologies are reducing the prospects of earning a living in the market-oriented economy. They will also help in obtaining a different way of thinking about wealth—the form of wealth that is not taxed and thus does not contribute to the purchase of weapons systems that are used to maintain the hegemony of Western capitalism.

Other questions need to be asked in these face-to-face conversations. How do the differences between life as a participating member of the cultural commons and life as a solitary worker in some part of the market economy affect a person's health? On average, are there fewer health issues experienced by people pursuing a craft and participating in networks of mutual support than what is encountered by people engaged in repetitive work, who are continually concerned about jobs lost to outsourcing or replacement by a labor-saving technology that yields a higher profit for the owner?

As the above examples suggest, the cultural commons are actual communities of mutual interest. It needs to be emphasized that in most instances the people who carry forward the traditions being identified here are less dependent upon a money economy and lead less environmentally destructive lives. They live within a very complex mix of people, ideologies, market/technological forces found in cities large and small, in suburbia, and in rural settings. They are also part of different ethnic cultures that influence what is carried forward as part of that culture's common wealth. The questions students need to ask of participants in these different cultural commons activities are the same, regardless of whether the person is largely alone in pursuing a tradition such as weaving, or using local materials to make musical instruments. Indeed, student ethnographies of mentors in the complex communities that set themselves apart from the strip malls across America may be even more important. These creative individuals and networks of mutual support represent what can be expanded upon as the combination of the ecological crisis and the displacement of workers by digital technologies create even greater stresses in society. These mentors are very much like the seeds of trees that sprout and start the process of new growth only after the ground cover has been burned.

HOW THIS PEDAGOGICAL MODEL APPLIES TO STUDENTS

A cultural commons curriculum that contributes to less environmentally destructive lifestyles also needs to engage students in learning about the modern forces that are enclosing what remains of the cultural commons. The forms of enclosure mentioned earlier include the technologies, ideologies, and silences that are central to the modern form of economic development and progress. The teacher's mediating role could be easily handled if she/he imposed upon the students an ideological framework that dismisses all aspects of the modern/scientific/technological/market/progress-at-all-cost as the source of the world's problems. This ideological framework might also lead to romanticizing the cultural commons in ways that preclude considering the prejudices and organized forms of terror that continue to be part of some cultural commons. We have to remember that the Ku Klux Klan was part of the cultural commons in communities spread across the country.

The non-ideological role of the teacher requires a different approach, one that is again grounded in an ecological framework that takes account of historical forces, deep cultural assumptions, and the impact made on natural systems and the ecologies referred to here as the cultural commons. This requires going beyond textbooks and the computer programmer's account by focusing on how these different aspects of the modernizing agenda impact daily cultural practices—which leads to bringing the students' descriptive accounts of actual cultural practices into the discussions.

Just as the curriculum focuses on cultural commons practices, mutual support networks, and mentors in the community, it also needs to focus on the different forms of enclosure. Providing students with the historical background on different forms of enclosure is likely to be a special challenge. It can be addressed by collaborating with faculty who have studied the cultural forces that gave rise to the dominant forms of enclosure, such as (i) print and the emphasis on literacy, (ii) traditions of thinking that marginalized the importance of studying the culture-transforming nature of different technologies, and (iii) the rise of market economies that led to undermining the craft guild systems. If this is not possible, the educator can encourage students to ask their own questions about the historical and cultural roots of different forms of enclosure. The naming of different forms of enclosure, such as private property, capitalism, technology, emancipation, and so forth, provides a starting point that connects with another area of the curriculum, namely, encouraging students to recognize that words have a history. Students can then trace the different meanings key words have had over time. Community elders can also be important to learning about the more recent history of different forms of enclosure. Interviews, including more open discussion sessions where elders feel free to share how their life experiences were influenced by different forms of enclosure (which will differ from culture to culture), will provide important insights that go beyond what can be learned from textbooks or educational software. The important point that needs emphasizing is that the process of enclosure has a history, and the form it took was largely influenced by the root metaphors (cultural assumptions) taken for granted at critical points in the history of the West. This historical/linguistic perspective is essential to recognizing that forms of enclosure are not based on universal truths or free of hidden cultural influences.

While gaining historical and cross-cultural understanding will be a work in process, it will provide a necessary corrective to so much of what is learned in both informal and formal educational settings, namely, the ways in which human/cultural authorship is hidden in much of what passes as knowledge. This latter includes the sciences and what they relegate to temporary zones of silence (until the scientific gaze is turned upon them. Another characteristic of current approaches to education also needs to be addressed in a cultural commons curriculum. That is, there is a long tradition of assuming that reading about an idea, theory, event, even a dynamic process, leads to understanding. What is often overlooked is that students bring different interpretive frameworks to what they read, and in many instances what they read or listen to is too abstract to be fully understood. This can be attributed to the cultural differences between the students' taken-for-granted world and the ways in which print and nouns undermine the emergent, relational, and co-dependent nature of life processes.

The problem is that even explanations by experts, by highly regarded scholars and artists with a special gift for sharing their deepest insights, and by computer programmers—even these are unable to overcome the many ways knowledge remains an abstraction. Instead of just reading or listening to different explanations of how different forms of enclosure are affecting the cultural commons, students need to expand upon these brief accounts with descriptive accounts of enclosure from their own daily experiences in the cultural commons. Again, doing ethnographies reinforces the practice of making explicit and giving close attention to the lived cultural patterns. Ethnography (which Clifford Geertz refers to as "thick description") also leads to developing the conceptual understandings and elaborated vocabularies necessary for communicative competence. The following are examples of what should be part of the curriculum. These can be introduced at different levels in the educational process—with older students being introduced to a more in-depth examination of the historical origins of enclosure patterns, including the earlier monetization of different cultural commons traditions.

PRINT AND DATA

Early uses of print in the West for commercial and military purposes, as well as its use by philosophers, social theorists, and those who transformed the oral traditions of Jews, Christians, and Muslims into sacred texts, can be used to make explicit both the important uses of this technology as well as its limitations. Its early commercial and military uses, as will become obvious to students, were important for keeping objective records that overcame the possible shortcomings of human memory and other human machinations. It would be important, though, for students to consider how some cultural groups still carry forward the tradition of orally based agreements—which has interesting implications in light of how anything now electronically communicated can be hacked.

In addition to how print and data cannot fully represent the emergent and relational nature of the information-rich ecologies within which students live (which students should discuss), the more immediate implications relate to how an uncritical use of print and data involves a shift in the form of knowledge that is prioritized. And this shift relates directly to the cultural bias that holds that print and data provide a more accurate and objective representation of reality than face-to-face communication—where the "subjectivity" scholars most fear might be expressed. The way for students to assess the accuracy of this cultural bias is to have them discuss the experiential differences between reading a manual on how to carry out a task and engaging in the task interpersonally with a mentor. Students should consider critical questions. While a printed manual may provide useful information and even a step-by-step guide for the task, does it also model for students how to exhibit different character qualities such as patience, empathy, or how to reinforce the Other while disagreeing with her/him? To engage their culturally mediated, emergent, and relational world, students should ask how social policies based on abstract theory (such as the idea that economic and technological globalization leads to the latest expression of progress) will affect the local economy. What role might this theory have on the prospect of having to engage in yet another war to protect the "American way of life"? (This in itself is another abstraction that affects how people think and speak.)

There are also questions about how print has contributed to the reification of earlier ways of thinking that now contribute to the enclosure of the cultural commons, such as the cultural/historical origins of the idea of private ownership of physical and cultural property. Given that the idea of private ownership is closely tied to the idea of the autonomous individual and the accumulation of material wealth, students should be encouraged to consider the differences in how both are understood within the context of the cultural commons. How, for example, is poverty understood if wealth is associated with possessing a skill or talent useful to others and a willingness to participate in mutually supportive activities? Unraveling the ecology of unsustainable ideas and vocabularies will be important to overcoming the current ways in which abstract thinking fails to take account of the range of experiences in the cultural commons.

THE ROLE OF LANGUAGE IN ENCLOSING THE CULTURAL COMMONS

Becoming aware of the many ways in which the cultural commons are being enclosed by the economic and technological forces that drive the West's approach to modernization also requires giving attention to how the meaning of words influences what is given attention, what is ignored, and how the interpretations associated with both lead to different behaviors and even social policies. What was discussed in earlier chapters—(i) the conduit/sender-receiver view of communication, (ii) how many current meanings of words were framed by the choice of analogs settled upon in the distant past, (iii) the role played by root metaphors in taken-for-granted interpretive frameworks, and (iv) the way English nouns reinforce an ontology of fixed entities rather than the emergent and relational world of cultural and natural ecologies—these also need to be part of a cultural commons curriculum.

The role language plays in the enclosure of the cultural commons will be easily recognized by students if they consider the widely held current meaning of the word "tradition." After students have examined how Enlightenment thinkers, as well as early scientists, settled upon the analogs that framed "tradition" as patterns of thinking and cultural practices that are sources of backwardness standing in the way of progress, they should then do an ethnography of the traditions they reenact on a daily basis. This process of naming traditions—from spelling and patterns of meta-communication to recipes, from the subject/verb/object pattern of thinking and writing to social justice practices and methods required by the scientific method—will also lead to an awareness that most traditions, even the prejudices and patterns of marginalization, are taken for granted. And because these experiences are a presupposed part of daily life, they are not likely to be recognized as traditions. Students should also identify traditions in the industrial/technological/consumer culture that need to be intergenerationally renewed, as well as those that are sources of exploitation and the overshooting the sustaining capacity of natural systems.

Consideration of how language both constitutes and hides reality is also important to understanding how the cultural commons of other cultures are enclosed This comparative framework could, in turn, lead to a reconsideration of the current relevance of traditions that have been identified as either dead or located so far in the past that they are no longer relevant. The medieval traditions of the craft guilds might be an example that has special relevance for the cultural commons located in heavily populated urban areas.

The meaning of other words and phrases framed by widely accepted analogs also needs to be reconsidered within the context of the cultural commons. These include "progress," "individualism," "intelligence," "wealth," "economy," and "ecological intelligence." The irony is that the intergenerational traditions of sharing skills, engaging in barter and mutual exchange systems, face-to-face accountability and decision-making (admittedly, along with unjust traditions, as well) can be traced back to the first humans. Yet the vocabularies contributing to the current enclosure of the cultural commons are based on the earlier experiences of people driven by hubris and the myth of unending progress.

IDEOLOGIES AND FUTURE PATHWAYS

The focus on ideologies is really an extension of the earlier discussion on how language contributes to the enclosure of the cultural commons. An ideology is a conceptual map for how society should be organized and what we should strive for in the future. A life guided by this system of ideals or set of myths leads to language that constructs the reality envisaged by the ideology. Vocabularies thus become critical to the political role of ideologies, with nonsupportive vocabularies being largely excluded. Modernizing ideologies, such as libertarianism, market liberalism, Marxism that has evolved into eco-socialism, and fascism rely heavily upon vocabularies that support the idea of progress and thus exclude words that refer to any redeeming value of the past. It is also important to note that in their original formulation they all excluded any reference to the environment as becoming a limiting factor on what could be achieved if the ideology were followed consistently.

As learning about different modernizing ideologies is only an elective option at the university level, it is unlikely that many students considering participation in the cultural commons will understand the difference between the cultural commons and these modernizing ideologies, given that the latter are now being updated to include references to environmental issues ("green-washed") in their guiding vocabularies. And the promoters of different ideologies will be increasingly active as evidence mounts that the 600-year experiment in economic and technologically driven progress, which has led to material, cultural, and spiritual impoverishment for the majority of the world's population, is coming to an end. As these modernizing ideologies increasingly dominate the media and political debates, whether they take account of the importance of the cultural commons or lead to policies that further enclose them will become even more important. Participants in the cultural commons thus need to know what sets these ideologies apart. This brief overview is intended to highlight the sources of danger as well as support for a cultural commons-centered lifestyle.

Libertarianism has its immediate conceptual roots in the thinking of Ayn Rand, but it is now reflected in policies promoted by the CATO Institute. The main focus of libertarian thinking is on the rights of individuals to pursue their economic self-interest in a capitalist-driven economy. This culturally uninformed view of what drives human behavior leads to limiting the role of government to the enforcement of contracts and providing for the nation's defense. Its role is not to redistribute wealth to those who have not succeeded in meeting life's challenges. Thus altruism and religious teaching about helping others have no place in determining the role of government. Rather, government should follow the rules of Social Darwinism: that is, it should provide as much as possible the tax-free environment that enables the strongest and most competitive to prevail.

There is nothing in Rand's writings or in the thinking of the CATO Institute about conserving habitats and species—or even that there is an ecological crisis. Nor are the cultural commons mentioned, and thus no warning about the dangers ahead of integrating what remains of the cultural commons into the market system. Because of the widespread misuse of our political vocabulary, libertarianism, which mirrors many of the populist values of the Tea Party movement, is usually identified as reflecting conservative thinking. The reality is that there is nothing that the proponents of this free market ideology want to conserve except the right to innovate, to compete, and to pursue, on a global scale, more profits.

Market liberalism is closely aligned with the core values of libertarianism, but its roots can be found in the thinking of classical Western philosophers such as John Locke, Adam Smith, René Descartes, Jeremy Bentham, and Herbert Spencer. More recent theorists include Friedrich von Hayek and Milton Friedman. Market liberalism is also more dependent upon the early tradition of scientific thinking that viewed the environment as an exploitable resource. It is also more supportive of technologies that lead to an increase in profits. While this ideology is often referred to as the modern expression of conservatism, it does not support (i) conserving craft knowledge, (ii) the rights of workers to organize, (iii) legislation that protects species and habitats, or (iv) the rights of other cultures to resist being colonized by the ideas and practices of market liberalism. In effect, the mythical, abstract, and thus ethnocentric thinking of classical liberal philosophers provides the conceptual and moral basis of their thinking. That is, the autonomous individual is their basic social unit, the environment is an endlessly exploitable resource, and technological innovations and market forces lead to a Social Darwinian interpretation of progress.

None of the following are supported by market liberalism: (i) intergenerational knowledge and skills (ii) patterns of mutual support and mentoring relationships, (iii) lifestyles that lead to a smaller ecological footprint, (iv) the accountability and moral reciprocity supported by face-to-face relationships, (v) the practice of local democracy, (vi) reliance upon technologies scaled to local environmental and human conditions, and (vii) an awareness of the value of self-limitation for the sake of future generations. Market liberalism, through its well-funded army of lobbyists, has made a sham of democratic decision-making. It promotes the digital revolution, which is overturning privacy, enabling hackers who threaten our basic securities, and contributing to the final subjugation of workers by replacing them with digital machines. That the media continues to refer to market liberals as conservatives is yet further evidence of how American higher education perpetuates the deep cultural assumptions that underlie the industrial/consumer-dependent lifestyle that will lead in upcoming decades to a crisis wherein nearly 9 billion people will be without adequate water, sources of protein, and work.

Marxism/eco-socialism may also contribute to the more heated conversations about ways to address the deepening ecological crisis—which the proponents of this position have now, at last, recognized. While participants in the various ethnic and community-centered local commons are actually withdrawing from the market economy by focusing their lives on the work at hand, Marxists/eco-socialists devote their energies to clarifying how they *think* about environmental issues, for example, the importance of the commons and the need to liberate workers from the ways they have been oppressed by the capitalist system. Most are university professors and thus carry forward a key characteristic of the academic mindset—which is to use their hyper-expanded language codes to provide brief overviews of all the reform movements such as Green Localism, Deep Ecology, Bio-regionalism, different national Green Parties, and to explain why they fall short in overthrowing capitalism. And like most academics who have not thought about how print reproduces the old ontology of a world of fixed entities, ideas, and group identities, they ignore how the thinking within these groups has changed over time. The totalitarian tendencies within this messianic group are better served by misrepresenting how other environmental groups are stuck in fixed positions. Like other forms of mythic thinking, a totalitarian mindset is dependent upon reducing the world to fixed abstractions.

The traditional Marxist roots of eco-socialism lead to viewing capitalism as the source of all forms of exploitation, but the revisionist eco-socialists do not address how the overthrow of capitalism is to occur. Murray Bookchin, an important theorist within this group, exhibits the quality of mind that puts other people and their ideas into the two categories eco-socialists are most comfortable with: that is, the group of friends who adhere to a narrow set of ideas, and the enemy, who, while well meaning, emphasize different ideas and strategies. Once, I was part of a conversation where Gregory Bateson's name came up, and Bookchin immediately labeled him a fascist.

The long-term goal of overthrowing capitalism, including the hybrid form of capitalism promoted by the Business Alliance for Local Living Economies, will require a radical shift in the deep cultural assumptions that most people take for granted, yet the eco-socialists do not address how to bring this about. Indeed, they are silent about the range of language issues that must be addressed if there is any hope of making the transition to an ecologically sustainable future. Nor do they consider the cultural differences between largely print-based and predominately oral cultures, and how the latter have developed sustainable forms of ecological intelligence. What I have found in my interactions with these theorists is that in order to maintain the incorrectness of all other cultural approaches to the ecological crisis, they deliberately misrepresent the Other's ideas and practices.

The Marxist/eco-socialists may appear supportive of the diversity of the cultural commons, but the combination of dogmatism and missionary spirit lead them to fail when it comes to the real test, which is to actually participate in carrying forward the intergenerational knowledge and skill that are the basis of communities that do find ways to withdraw from dependency on the industrial/consumer-dependent lifestyle. Like the other ideologies that still carry forward the misconceptions of Enlightenment thinkers, they assume that progress depends upon a combination of critical thinking and even revolution itself. The problem is that revolution is a metaphor whose meaning changes depending on the choice of analogs. Writing books on the need to overthrow capitalism and about the misguided efforts of those who do address the ecological crisis seem more appropriate to these academic radicals than putting their lives (and retirement benefits) on the line by charging the police barricades and destroying the elite class that controls the means of production. Revolution can also mean promoting the digital revolution that is changing the conceptual foundations of life. Eco-socialism is an ideology that will continually transform itself at the theoretical level, which will add to the list of apostates while at the same time alienating other groups that are actually addressing local alternatives to the globalizing agenda of the industrial revolution.

Fascism, unlike the other modernizing ideologies, will not be promoted by easily recognized spokespersons, as is the case with the other modernizing ideologies. Yet, like the fascism of Mussolini's Italy and Nazi Germany, the culture-transforming agenda that is already spreading through all levels of American society is based on a combination of mythic thinking, transforming technologies, blind faith in market capitalism, and the unquestioned assumption of the progressive destiny of American society. Fascism, as Benito Mussolini understood it, achieves strength through society-wide conformity to a common set of values and social vision. To achieve the necessary level of conformity, the Italian, German, and other promoters of this ideology, had to develop a network for keeping people's ideas, behaviors, and associations under constant surveillance. And there had to be centralized governmental agencies in close cooperation with various police enforcement groups that oversaw the entire array of surveillance technologies. The digital revolution that is seen as contributing to so many benefits in different sectors of society, and where the average person has willingly given up the right to privacy and security from hackers in order to enjoy the convenience of digital technologies, has now led to a near total surveillance culture. And with advances in wireless communication and the spread of the Internet of Things into every aspect of daily life, the behavioral information that has so far escaped being monitored will become available. Agencies will create data profiles on personal behaviors, and data scientists will take their orders from heads of governmental agencies who will define what constitutes terrorism.

As more of the educational process is computer-mediated, it will lead to curricula and computer testing that can easily be monitored for political correctness. The current alliance of (i) scientists focused on monitoring brain functions and how to change consciousness with chemicals, (ii) computer experts working to develop artificial intelligence that will take over from humans, (iii) corporations ever in search of new markets, and (iv) military self-interest which continues to align itself with corporate agendas — this alliance will assert itself more directly as social chaos threatens to spread in response to the failure of natural systems. This was the same alliance, in spite of their differences in guiding mythologies, that supported the fascism of both Italy and Nazi Germany.

The surveillance and police state infrastructure are already in place, and the mis-education of most Americans has left them without the conceptual basis for recognizing how far down the pathway to a fascist future we have already traveled — all in name of progress and national security. One of the virtues of the cultural commons is that it represents a different form of resistance to modernizing movements. And it is likely to be ignored by the proponents of the different yet closely aligned modernizing ideologies. In not being as fully dependent upon the digital/market system, the forms of resistance to a full-blown fascist future can be found in pursuing lives less dependent on technology and consumerism. In not contributing to the further degradation of natural systems that will lead to social unrest, the cultural commons lifestyle will quietly represent a different political model that will remind people of what is being lost — and what is still possible — even as social unrest spreads.

Organic Marxism, a new potential pathway being developed by Philip Clayton and Justin Heinzeker, suggests a partnership between process and socialist philosophies, with adaptations to both in order to respond more explicitly to the environmental crisis. As Heinzekehr writes, their goal is

> not to return to any "original" framework or to foster a new Marxist or Whiteheadian orthodoxy. Rather, we conceive the process and socialist traditions as existing within a constant process of reinterpretation, re-application, and revision. Reading these traditions in the context of a commitment to ecological sustainability, we discover a socialism that leads us

beyond mechanical orthodoxy toward grassroots engagement. We find a process-based understanding of systems that functions not merely as an abstract description of reality, but as an effective critique of economic domination and a lever for social change. (2016)

The theoretical side of Organic Marxism finds practical expression in alliances with the De-Growth and Occupy movements, cultural commons movements within African American communities, and the Sustainability Revolution.

Bio-cultural conservatism represents an interpretative framework that takes account of how cultural practices affect the ability of natural systems to reproduce themselves. In effect, conserving habitats, species, and larger systems such as the earth's soil, aquifers, streams, and oceans is essential if human life is to continue. We are already conserving many cultural traditions that are not recognized because we re-enact them on a taken-for-granted basis. The problem is knowing which traditions to intergenerationally renew and which traditions to reject (such as beliefs and practices that lead to free markets, to technologies that subordinate human well-being for the sake of profits, to language that encodes the misconceptions of the past, and so forth). Because of the unthinking ways in which traditions are re-enacted, conserving is integral to all aspects of the cultural ecologies in which we live, including the ecology of language, technology, the arts, craft skill and knowledge, politics, and so forth. Each has a history, and because of the emergent and relational ontology that characterizes all ecological systems, the challenge is not learning how to conserve. Rather, it is in knowing what needs to be conserved to strengthen self-reliant and morally coherent communities that enable members to share in the wealth of the cultural commons.

That bio-cultural conservatism helps to clarify the pathway to an eco-logically sustainable future can be seen more clearly when compared to the modernizing ideologies derived from the abstract theories of Western ethnocentric philosophers and social theorists who ignored different forms of cultural intelligence and adopted the myth of a human-centered world. Bio-conservatism also finds support among political theorists who were critics of modernity. These conservative thinkers include Edmund Burke, who was critical of organizing society on the basis of abstract ideas which emphasized a form of individualism that ignored continuities between past, present, and future. Michael Oakshott's *Rationalism in Politics* (1991) warned against emphasis on the rational organization of work that elevates concern with efficiency and profits over the human need for mastering a craft and engaging in community-strengthening activities. Matthew Crawford's focus on the personal and social nature of pursuing a craft that re-connects with traditions, with the value of social usefulness, and with interactions with the physical world, is very much in the Oakshott tradition of conservatism. Perhaps the best examples of bio-cultural conservative writers today are Wendell Berry and Vandana Shiva. People who are conscious promoters of intergenerational knowledge and skills that strengthen communities, and who are aware that the cultural commons have a smaller adverse impact on natural systems, are living bio-conservative lives.

As the everyday ecologies of ongoing conversations and media talk continually mislabel the various expressions of libertarianism and market liberalism as conservative, it is important to challenge this drift into the Orwellian world of doublespeak that totalitarianism relies upon. Many people who lack a background understanding of different ideologies, and who want to conserve their taken-for-granted traditions, may assume that their interests will be protected by supporting the misnamed conservatives. This is where we need to recognize that politics begins with how language is being misused, and that the exercise of democracy begins with naming relationships, values, and practices correctly. This also applies to how we use such words as individualism and progress.

⮞ 9 ⮜

Is the Digital Revolution Sowing the Seeds of
a Techno-Fascist Future?

B EFORE CRITICIZING THE TITLE OF THIS CHAPTER as excessively alarmist, compare the guiding ideology of the digital revolution, as well as the cultural changes it has already introduced, to the
characteristics of fascism. It is also important to recognize that fascism
varies between cultures. Italian fascism was different in several important ways from German fascism, and if Oswald Moseley had come to
power in Great Britain, his brand of hyper-nationalism would have dif-
fered—just as the fascism of France's Jean-Marie Le Pen, as it evolves,
will be imprinted with what is distinctively French. The same holds
for the early signs of techno-fascism, the chief characteristics of which
suggest a more international and thus less distinctly American model.

The connections between technologies (digital, especially) and
fascism are not widely recognized, partly because fascism is mostly
understood by looking through the rearview mirror of recent historical
events. Technologies were essential to the short-lived successes of both
Italian and German fascism, but both were also driven by the social
unrest following the end of World War I, racial mythologies (especially
for the Germans), the lack of well-established democratic institutions,
and the economic turmoil of worldwide depression. Techno-fascism is

characterized by the way more aspects of daily life are becoming dependent upon digital technologies. This leads to many benefits, but at the same time, digital technologies not only reduce the diversity in cultural ways of knowing; they also increasingly subordinate human thought and behaviors to the dictates of machines. Unlike the racist mythologies of German fascism, the mythic dimensions of techno-fascism are rooted in ancient religious narratives about humans naming and taking control of the environment, and in the abstract thinking of philosophers who laid the conceptual and moral foundations for the modern myth of progress—which includes the idea that human life is mechanistic and driven by Nature's laws governing natural selection. While the moral foundations of techno-fascism align with the values of market capitalism and the progress-oriented ideology of a science that easily slips into scientism, its level of efficiency and totalitarian potential can easily lead to repressive systems that will not tolerate dissent—especially on the part of those challenging how the colonizing nature of techno-fascism is destroying the environment and alternative cultural lifestyles.

The primary characteristic of all fascist modernizing movements is conformity of thinking and behavior, which is directed and controlled by total surveillance systems that track and keep records of people's thoughts, behaviors, and relationships. The latest in the emerging techno-fascist arsenal of surveillance technologies is the facial recognition system being adopted by local police—which will shortly become part of the FBI's one billion dollar Next Generation Identification Program. Thus, photos of people not suspected of criminal activities, as well as those who are, will be instantly available to 18,000 local, state, federal, and international law enforcement agencies. Facial recognition technology can identify 16,000 distinct features of a person's face and compare them with other photos held by police agencies at a rate of more than one million faces per second.

Three of the most important threats to what remains of our civil liberties include: (i) facial recognition software has a 20 percent failure rate (ii) social unrest resulting from extreme environmental changes can easily lead to redefining what constitutes criminal behavior, and (iii) police biases and misinterpretations lead to police actions that result in the deaths of innocent people (a problem now plaguing local police across the country).

In spite of how human biases influence the interpretation of data and images, a characteristic of fascism shared with the market system is the quest for new technologies that make tracking people and their market preferences more efficient. Writing in the *New York Times* (9/25/15), John Eligon and Timothy Williams note that corporations are also turning to what in policing circles is called predictive analytics and data mining. The key word that bothers civil libertarians is "predictive," as it suggests that police and other national security agencies are gathering data on people's behavior even though they have not committed a crime. As Eligon and Williams note, the Chicago police have developed a "heat list" of 400 people who are considered more likely than the average citizen to become engaged in a violent crime. The economic, political, and social stresses that will accompany the breakdown in natural systems, and the civil wars fought over the increasing scarcity of water and other resources, will lead to greater police efforts to assert central control, especially over the critics of government policies that favor the rich and politically powerful. Criminality, as we witnessed in the fascist regimes of the last century, can be redefined to include those who challenge the fascist drift of the country. Predictive analytics is already leading to a list of professors regarded as radical and thus subversive, including professors who are thought to be sympathetic to the idea of a Palestinian State.

Increased reliance upon computer-mediated learning at all levels of education contributes to the conformity of thinking needed in a techno-fascist state. Lost are the ethnically diverse intergenerational narratives passed forward through face-to-face relationships, which leaves students exposed only to myths that serve the interests of the controlling elites: scientists, computer scientists/engineers, corporate heads, and a military establishment increasingly concerned that the ecological crisis will disrupt its hegemonic agenda. The guiding ideology and moral codes were first articulated in the early 17th century by Johannes Kepler, who suggested that life processes should be understood as machine-like. This notion continues to be reinforced by computer scientists who have announced the beginning of the post-biological world—and their followers—who rely on the values of efficiency, accountability, profit, data, and purposive rationality to engineer machines that replicate human behaviors and thought processes (their own, of course).

Learning programs reflect the presuppposed world of the people who write the software. This presupposed world already includes the practice of relying upon print and data to communicate the false sense of a factual and objective account of social events and ideas (as though the interpretative frameworks of writer and reader have no influence on what is written or represented as data). Given the above, there is less chance that students will recognize that the words appearing in print are metaphors encoding the thought processes of earlier generations—people who were unaware of environmental limits. In short, conformity of thinking relies upon (i) a mix of mythologies, (ii) the elimination of historical/cultural memories that do not support these guiding myths, and (iii) vocabularies that limit thought and thus awareness that the technological/economic/industrial/military elites have set an agenda for everyone to follow.

Questions that need to be asked about parallels between the European varieties of fascism and American rightwing groups include the following: Is there a parallel between how the German National Socialists in the 1930s manipulated democratic process to gain support of their totalitarian agenda and how the U. S. National Rifle Association uses the protection of the Constitution and congressional campaign contributions to support its agenda of arming rightwing hyper-patriotic Americans who stand ready to intervene should a peace movement break out across the country? What about the parallels between the male-dominated fascist movements in Europe and the male-dominated fields of computer science, engineering, national security agencies, the military establishment, and corporations whose future is tied to the digital revolution? Does a concern with data, efficiency, and a vision of progress easily interpreted in the language of Social Darwinism reflect the West's deep assumption that this is a human-centered universe which should be guided by the scientific rationalism of men? Are the roots of violence, especially toward women, traceable to the monotheistic religions in the West, where God is associated with masculine (so interpreted) qualities?

But fascism also relies upon the combination of conformity in thought and values, of loss of historical memory, and a of perceived crisis or endpoint that requires the collective energy and loyalty of young and old. In addition, there needs to be a significant percentage of the population that is hyper-patriotic, thinks in clichés, and is willing to support the use of imprisonment and torture of those who challenge the rise of techno-fascism — especially those labeled as environmentalists — who will be viewed, as were the Jews in Nazi Germany, as weakening the power of the state.

Digitally mediated learning, which is heavily dependent upon print- and data-based accounts that encode the cultural assumptions and ideologies of the people who write the programs, reinforces a mindset that responds to short explanations. Already, boredom is associated with long explanations and written accounts. The ways in which social media reinforces the importance of an ever-shifting sense of immediacy and instant response to anonymous Others ensures that the emergence of a fascist state will go unrecognized. The increased reliance on mobile devices has led to the coining of a new word, "micromoment." This is now understood by the cutting-edge advertising industry as the current length of time they have to bring a product or service to the attention of a potential consumer. The understanding within the industry is that a potential consumer's attention span is eight seconds. The ultimate goal is to get the information on a product or service to appear on a mobile device the moment it occurs to the potential customer as a need.

The shortening of attention spans and the expectation that there is an instant answer to fulfill personal needs should be understood within the larger context that takes account of impacts on natural systems, historical memories of social justice traditions, the growing disparities between vast numbers living in poverty and the super-rich, and the social tensions that will rise exponentially as environmentalists challenge those who have an economic and ideological interest in denying the existence of the ecological crisis. Those in denial have a vested interest in how techno-fascism continues to shape human consciousness to equate progress with even higher levels of efficiency, personal conveniences, and allowing constant monitoring by medical experts of one's bodily functioning and appearance.

The totalitarian nature of the digital revolution can be seen in the proliferation of apps that represents both a hyper-growth industry and a personal quest for quick riches on the part of younger people who are part of the growing contingent workforce (now a third of employed Americans). They must rely upon their own economic efforts now that the old system of lifelong employment, with its broken system of social contracts, is fast disappearing. The drive is to compete with others in creating an app that attracts so many users that it leads to great wealth and thus banishes the anxiety of becoming economically destitute in later years. After all, safety nets cannot be justified in the monoculture emerging from the integration of techno-fascism and libertarian/market liberalism. This new growth market, like the gold rush in California, does not draw the reflective and ecologically informed, but rather those who want to develop the app that will be the panacea for those who want to get on the technology bandwagon. The ways in which techno-fascism is overwhelming individual, historically and even ecologically informed judgments can be seen in the number of apps for improving math instruction, reading, teaching in other curricular areas, and classroom management. There are more than 3900 school-related apps, so many that school districts now rely upon external experts to guide them on the merits and uses of apps.

Nearly every aspect of personal and social life can now be organized and monitored by anonymous experts who lack any historical knowledge of how to live a more ecologically sustainable and community-centered life. Deep knowledge of local contexts, cultural differences, intergenerational knowledge, the importance of personal memory, critical judgment, and wisdom traditions from the past, are not part of the life-world of the generation raised by spending hours in the abstract and individually centered world of digital culture. Like other forms of cultural reproduction, they simply reproduce the taken-for-granted way progress is understood within the emergent techno-fascist culture that is now being celebrated (i) in the media, (ii) in people's economic behaviors, (iii) by politicians supporting the NRA, and (iv) by the mega-corporations that control major segments of American life and are major forces behind the denial that there is an ecological crisis.

The face-to-face systems of local control involving a variety of democratic practices and traditions of ecological wisdom, and which often involve religious and indigenous communities, are under threat from (i) the abstract knowledge read on a computer screen, and (ii) from the myth of individual decision-making in the unlimited world of data. Where in the digitally mediated curriculum will students learn about the ecologically sustainable traditions of their communities? Where will they learn of past mistakes? The ideology underlying the digital revolution represents traditions, including local decision-making, as a source of backwardness and an impediment to students creating their own ideas from the wealth of context-free data available on the Internet.

It is even becoming difficult to recognize the differences between local activism focused on social justice issues and the way corporations such as Coca-Cola, Wal Mart, Chick-fil-A, and health insurers (organizers of the "town hall" protests against President Obama's health care legislation) now use social media to engage in what is called "astroturfing." This is the term used to distinguish between genuine grassroots social justice movements and the supposedly "grassroots" groups created by corporations to advance their economic agendas. Corporations regularly deflect criticism of their harmful products by using pseudo science and social media to create the impression that a wide segment of the public supports them. For example, Coca Cola has spent millions funding the Global Energy Balance Network, which is headed by scientists who claim that lack of exercise and not the sugar content of soft drinks is the cause of obesity. Putting profits above the well-being of the public is yet another way in which many American corporations emulate German corporations in the 1930s that supported the transition from a weakened democracy to the militant and expansionist vision of National Socialism under Hitler. Indeed, a number of prominent American corporations such as Ford, Kodak, Coca Cola, and Standard Oil were essential to the German war effort, along with BMW, Siemens, and Bayer. Many American youth now identify the last three named as American companies.

Digital technologies now have indispensible uses that range across a wide range of cultural activities, from medicine, scientific research, monitoring and maintaining the society's technological and economic infrastructure, education, and nearly every facet of the industrial/consumer-dependent culture. But digital technologies have also introduced irreversible cultural changes, such as undermining local democracy (did we vote for any of these technologies?), creating a new generation that is unaware of the political dangers and threats to personal security that accompany the loss of privacy. They have undermined the (i) face-to-face intergenerational narratives essential to maintaining ethnic identities and (ii) traditions of the cultural commons that strengthen patterns of mutual support while reducing dependency upon consumerism. They have further strengthened the long-standing tradition in the West of elevating abstract knowledge over ecologically informed ways of thinking. Digital media is shortening people's attention span to the point where little more than slogans and sound bites serve as the basis of political decision-making. Following the standard set by Fox News of masking disinformation as a model of factual accuracy and objective reporting, millions of Americans have been conditioned to accept ideologically driven propaganda, which further reduces the likelihood of mass resistance to the techno-fascist agenda.

The fashion industry has never been on the side of conserving natural resources, but has always been in the forefront of pushing high-status, wealth-driven images of how successful people should dress. As both the design and use of materials promoted by the fashion industry send powerful messages about what should be valued and thus emulated within the larger society, the growing number of human-like robots has inspired fashion trendsetters to dress humans in ways that suggest the older, more mechanistic appearing robots. With the line that separates humans from robots becoming increasingly blurred, the message in the futurist film, *Ex Machina*, which might have sparked resistance to the computer scientists' understanding of progress, is likely to be lost. The comely female-bot outwits the highly gifted employee of a software company and then disappears into the flow of street traffic without leaving a hint of her non-biological origins. The robot was not only more beautiful but more intelligent and crafty than the humans who created her.

The critical question is whether there will be resistance to how everyday lives are being increasingly monitored, motivated to pursue the increasingly narrow economic agenda of the emerging techno-fascist culture, and stripped of historical values and identity. Will enough of the public recognize the dangers that lie ahead? Will they be able to articulate the importance of what is being lost? It is important to note that the computer scientists who play a central role in articulating the ideology that underlies the emerging techno-fascist culture totally ignore the deepening ecological crisis. The title of the book written by Peter Diamandis and Stephen Kotler, *Abundance: The Future is Better than You Think* (2012) could serve as the anthem as we march into the future envisioned by techno-fascists. It bears repeating: the scientific justification for replacing humans and their diverse cultures with the culture created by super-intelligent computers, according to a number of computer scientists following the lead of Ray Kurzweil (1999, 2005, 2012), is simply the process of natural selection.

Traditional defenses against totalitarian regimes are now being lost. To understand this, we need to focus more specifically on the cultural transformations that occur in the classroom. Here, students increasingly spend more of their day in computer-mediated learning, which displaces face-to-face interaction with teachers who might spark their curiosity to explore beyond the orthodoxies of the day. The many hours daily spent texting friends, playing video games, and exploring the seemingly endless realms of cyberspace also shortens attention spans in ways that undermine long-term memory. Speed and context-free slogans have now replaced depth of understanding and critical judgment. The same shift to computer-mediated thinking and communication is occurring in work settings, and in nearly every other venue in society—including vacation time. The current business ethos is for managers to constantly monitor how employees spend their time, including how quickly they perform different tasks. The panoptican system that Jeremy Bentham designed for keeping prisoners under constant surveillance is now being electronically extended to the office and other workplaces.

A brief review of previous chapters will bring out the cultural changes undermining democracy and ethnic difference, changes that are leading to the monoculture of digital consciousness.

PRINT, DATA, AND ABSTRACT THINKING

Print is unable to represent the emergent, relational, and co-dependent nature of biological and cultural ecologies, whether it is the multiple message systems being communicated as one walks through an open meadow, or interaction with honors students who argue that their ideas are original even though they have read a number of articles explaining how the analogs that frame the meaning of words they takesfor granted were settled upon in earlier eras. A printed account of the emergent, relational, and co-dependent behaviors in both the natural and cultural ecologies, especially if they are personal experiences, would provide only a surface and static (and thus abstract) account. What gets recorded in print is also influenced by the writer's biases, presupposed ways of understanding, and interpretative frameworks. These will all go unrecognized due to past socialization. The printed (also spoken) word relies upon a conduit (sender/receiver) view of language, which too often leads to ignoring that words have a history that influences what the reader will or will not be aware of.

The printed word, data, and oral communication that is influenced by the abstractions of the printed word shift attention away from the ongoing, embodied, and face-to-face experiences with others in the community. We are conditioned to accept as real the abstract accounts of what is happening in society. Bombarded daily from the media with threats and proposals for change, we become indifferent about assessing the accuracy of these claims and are thus easily led to think and value what fits the agenda of the controlling elites. The printed word, in effect, diverts attention away from the relational, emergent, and co-dependent nature of face-to-face and culturally mediated experiences.

For those who promote the worldview of a totally digitized future, the mythic thinking that merges the idea of progress with the meta-narrative of natural selection enables them to represent themselves as oracles of Nature's and the culture's destiny. Both become powerful sources of authority, especially when people's privacy, employment, sense of history, and cultural identity are monitored by the flood of sensors being introduced into every aspect of daily life.

The political importance of "connectivity," which computer scientists view as a strength of digital technologies, is largely unrecognized by the general public. Without it, the massive amount of data gathered on people's lives would not be so widely distributed to the various agencies — from producers of goods and services to the National Security Agency and other governmental agencies.

An ideology that drives the unrelenting quest to digitize every aspect of human experience represents the future as leading to improvements over the past. A state of consciousness wherein the expectation of a better future becomes dominant leads in turn to ignoring (i) traditions that are sources of everyday empowerment, and (ii) hard-won institutionalized ways of protecting one's civil liberties. When the past is no longer viewed as a mix of prejudices and social justice achievements, the depth and complexity of everyday experiences becomes narrowed and simplified by the limitations of what can represented in print and digitized forms.

As the Internet of Things leads to the wireless connectivity of all aspects of people's personal lives with everything else in the environment, the experience of being constantly watched may lead to a sense of security. But even small incidents should be taken as a warning that computer scientists have created, all in the name of progress, an interconnected policing system. A case in point: a typing error in one number of my house address by one agency led to the same error being repeated in mailings from a variety of governmental agencies and corporations wanting to promote their products. Now that this kind of connectivity is increasingly being used to anticipate acts of terrorism, or where crimes will occur, perhaps it is time to stop referring to this as surveillance and call it what it is: a policing system

The next step will be to monitor potential sources of dissent — a problem that scientists are now working on as they study the connections between people's vocabularies and their patterns of thinking.

Other scientists are making progress along the same pathway pioneered by Nazi scientists in developing facial recognition technologies. There are current efforts to discover the chemical changes needed to eliminate bad memories, which, then, can also be used to eliminate good memories (such as privacy and a life free of commercialism). Other efforts range from trying to extend Lee M. Silver's technologies for bio-engineering babies with traits wanted by their parents to engineering the conceptually and morally compliant babies needed in a techno-fascist state.

One of the ways that techno-fascism spreads throughout society like an unrecognized virus is that its supporting language relies heavily upon metaphors that are reassuring to many people. Most Americans support "progress," "security," "conservatism," "Americanism," and "patriotism." When they lack the conceptual background (thanks to omissions in our educational systems) they are unlikely to recognize that the so-called conservatives are actually a mix of libertarian and market liberals, and that the above metaphors have been used to justify imperialist-driven wars.

The expansion of surveillance of people's lives adds another layer to the fascist political agenda of the American rightwing that mirrors key characteristics of European fascism. This social agenda includes (i) placing barriers in people's ability to vote, (ii) using the prison system to control a large segment of the poor and non-white population, (iii) the intertwining of fundamentalist religions and segments of the government focused on national security, (iv) using the military to globalize the American way, (v) suppressing basic human rights, especially for women, (vi) undermining the rights of workers to organize, and (vii) enabling fraudulent elections where the super-wealthy are able to control the outcome of state and federal elections.

The expansion of technological and corporate power involves greater reliance upon the use of context-free metaphors such as "national security" and "terrorist" to justify using the power of the police against individuals and social groups engaged in demonstrations and acts of resistance against corporations that continue to have a destructive impact on the environment and peoples' lives. As sources of protein become even more limited due to the warming and acidification of the oceans, as droughts reduce the viability of genetically engineered seeds (and companies such as Monsanto reduce the variety of seeds in order to increase farmers' dependence), and many other scenarios that will be played out as ecological systems collapse, greater social unrest will occur in response to a variety of issues that the money-controlled state and federal governments have not addressed.

Social unrest will be further exacerbated as new digital technologies continue to reduce the need for workers, and as youth remain unaware of the political economy of the cultural commons where talents and patterns of mutual support lead to non-monetized forms of wealth. This is when the all-encompassing digital infrastructure will be used to suppress all forms of dissent—while at the same time relying upon metaphors that suggest police state tactics are intended to provide security in an increasing chaotic world. As the deepening ecological crisis and the displacement of humans by machines increases, techno-fascism will become the new normal.

ONLINE COURSES AND DEGREES

Changes are occurring so rapidly that we seem unable to connect the dots. Recent insights into how language issues are related to the ecological crisis have not yet become a widespread concern, with the result that the mythical thinking encoded in many of our guiding metaphors still goes unchallenged. When only the important, indeed indispensable, uses of print and data are understood, then little attention is given to how the merging of these technologies is changing the deep conceptual foundations of consciousness.

Also, the understanding of fascism by most Americans is limited to the short newsreel images of the World War II era—if even that. Few understand that it is a modernizing ideology, and that it relies upon myths. These now include yet another Social Darwinian interpretation that emphasizes, according to computer futurist writers Gregory Stock, Ray Kurzweil, and George Dyson, the transition to a post-biological world governed by super-intelligent computers.

Given this widely shared state of consciousness, promoting an even greater reliance upon using computers at all levels of public and higher education is understood as necessary to progress—even as digital technologies are radically changing the prospects of earning a living and taking for granted that the past has been made totally irrelevant. As soon as the pre-online generations die off, what remains of historical memory will depend upon the programmers' and data scientist's taken-for-granted world, which will be restricted by the way their field of graduate study excluded the need to understand the complexity of the cultures into which their digital technologies are introduced.

The dots we now need to connect include what will *not* be learned online, and how that in turn will contribute to (i) not being able to recognize the cultural/linguistic roots of the ecological crisis, (ii) not knowing alternatives to the near total dependence on a consumer lifestyle that is leading to ecological collapse, and (iii) not recognizing that the migration of millions of people from areas no longer able to support life will be magnified many times over as extreme weather, rising ocean levels, resource wars, and technologies further displace the need for workers.

Online courses and now online degrees offered by universities, ranging from the ever-present degree mills to elite universities, have many advantages. They are more convenient in terms of meeting a wider range of student income and family needs. And the need to attract students has led to aligning course requirements more closely to different career paths—which means that technical knowledge is prioritized over courses that would provide students a more critically informed historical and cultural perspective.

Perhaps the most important source of empowerment essential to resisting the conformity required by a techno-fascist regime is the ability to recognize and reframe, in terms of current cultural and ecological understandings, the many forms of metaphorical thinking that reproduce the assumptions and silences of earlier eras. Understanding and, better yet, participating in the mutually supportive lifestyles of the cultural commons represents ways of resisting the environmentally destructive commercialism that is central to techno-fascism. In effect, online education repeats the shortcomings of bricks-and-mortar public schools and universities.

School gardens and recycling practices fall far short of the cultural issues classroom teachers should be addressing, particularly since students in the early grades will be living, in 50 years or so, through the early stages of social unrest that will turn more violent in an already over-militarized world. Similarly, online university courses and degrees, still driven by the hubris that has become endemic among academics focused on overturning all traditions even though they are unaware of how many of them are sources of personal empowerment, will continue to perpetuate the Ponzi scheme of keeping up enrollments by promising to prepare students for careers even as the careers are being taken over by algorithms and robots.

If one only considers how public schools and most aspects of higher education continue to ignore Albert Einstein's warning about using the same mindset to correct today's problems that was used in creating them, as well as how far down the pathway of techno-fascism we have already travelled, it would seem there is little hope for the future. But as suggested in earlier chapters, the hope for the future can be seen in the cultural commons activities that need to become more widely recognized as sites of resistance, as well as community-centered lifestyles that rely upon democratic decision-making. These face-to-face communities are also less prone to electronic surveillance and thus less dependent upon the technologies essential to the control systems required in a techno-fascist state.

The next chapter will address the grass roots alternatives being explored in different regions of the world for passing forward the intergenerational knowledge and skills essential to strengthening the cultural commons—that now go by such different labels as the localism movement, transition communities, cooperative movements, and the revitalization of indigenous identities and cultures.

❧ 10 ❧

Change and Radical Transformation

by Marcus Ford

INSTITUTIONS, INCLUDING UNIVERSITIES, are always changing, but most of the changes are additive, piecemeal, and often superficial and ephemeral. Change is commonplace. Transformative change is exceedingly rare.

There is literally no end to the ways in which the modern liberal arts college and the modern university can change while remaining essentially the same—that is committed to the current social order, the Western worldview, and the same understanding of the purpose of higher education. Change on this level is of little importance. The case for fundamental change in higher education—radical or transformative change—rests on the belief that the current social order is unfair and unsustainable, that the modern scientific worldview is only partially correct (which is to say is not true), and that the current understanding of the purpose of higher education is too narrow. There is considerable evidence to support all of these judgments.

The **University of Phoenix**, the **Minerva Project**, **Udacity,** and **Coursera**, are sometimes lifted up as transformational developments in higher education. They are not. None challenges the dominant social order, the modern scientific worldview, or the purpose of higher education. They call into the question the viability of the public university, but not its objectives. They are different means to the same end.

The **University of Phoenix** was established in 1972 to meet the vocational needs of non-traditional students. It succeeded because it had no real competition, because of the "computer revolution," and because of its limited objectives (it chose not to engage in research, in extracurricular activities, or in those aspects of undergraduate education meant to help young people mature into responsible adulthood). Its mission was simply to help working people earn a diploma without giving up their job.

Minerva seeks to compete in another segment of the "education market." Minerva, which admitted its first class in 2014, aims to be the first online, elite liberal arts college. Offering all of its classes only online, it can, it claims, offer students both more personal attention and more freedom, and it can do so for less money. Minerva hopes to attract the same caliber of students who would otherwise choose to go to the most exclusive (and most expensive) private schools.

Udacity and **Coursera** represent yet another innovation in higher education made possible by new communication technology — but they do not challenge the fundamental objective of higher education in modern society. They are a factor in the changing landscape of higher education made possible by new modes of technology and by political shifts away from public education (or at least the funding of higher education), but they do not constitute transformation.

The University of Phoenix, Minerva, Udacity, and Coursera all claim to have built a better mouse trap, but the fact is — they are all mouse traps. None seeks to transform higher education. They are simply different ways of doing what we are already doing.

The **Swaraj Movement**, on the other hand, is an example of radical or transformative change in higher education. The Swaraj, or self-rule, movement rests on Gandhi's rejection of certain aspects of Western civilization, especially its extreme individualism, industrialism, and the notion "might makes right." In Gandhi's view, India needed to free itself not simply from British political rule but from the worldview and the values introduced into India by the British. What Gandhi realized is that Western-style higher education is not value-free or metaphysically neutral as it claims to be, instead, Western-style institutions of higher education reflect and reproduce Western beliefs and values.

The Swaraj movement in India is not simply a different way of accomplishing the same educational ends as Western-style education. It is an educational movement that challenges the metaphysics of Western-style education, challenges the dominant social order, and challenges what we mean by being human and how we should lead our lives together. Manish Jain's **People's Institute for Rethinking Education and Development** is one example of Gandhi's call for educational self-rule.

The newly established **Global University** is another example of radical educational reform or "transformation" as opposed to "change." The Global University, and the many schools associated with it, constitutes a radical departure from mainstream, Western higher education, because it problematizes what we mean by knowledge, and because it embraces the values associated with traditional ways of being: localism, sustainability, "radical democracy," and emancipation. Knowledge, from this perspective, is not value free. The purpose of higher education is not simply to collect data or to promote the current economic system; it is to promote personal well-being in a cultural tradition that has proven itself to be sustainable.

According to its website, the Global University "*will help bring into connection, interaction, and interrogation various experiences and wisdoms from the South and the North, from diverse sectors (labour, peasant, landless, women, indigenous, minorities…), from multiple movements and networks (on peace, ecology, justice, economy, philosophy, culture, feminism, liberation theology…)* all for the purpose of making life diverse, sustainable, and just. In short, in contrast to the modern university that seeks to advance modernity (and in the process obliterate non-modern ways of being), the Global University is committed to a future that allows for a great variety of cultures and ecosystems.

Flagstaff College, a small private college that does not yet exist, is also an example of transformational change in higher education.

Flagstaff College has certain affinities with both the Swaraj movement and the Global University. Like the Swaraj movement, it rejects the concepts of extreme individualism, industrialism, and "might makes right," and, like the Global University, it understands Western "expert knowledge" as problematic and less than fully true. Flagstaff College, however, comes to these positions by way of its commitment to the process-relational worldview developed by Alfred North Whitehead that has its roots in modern science and radical empiricism.

As currently envisioned, Flagstaff College will be a micro-college with only one major—sustainability, understood to mean not merely biological survival but also personal and social flourishing. At least initially, it will be a two-year "senior college" (limited to the last two years of an undergraduate degree) as opposed to a two-year junior college. Students who have not completed their Associates of Arts degree can do so through the local community college. All classes will be small and human-to-human; some will be action oriented.

Private colleges, once the norm in higher education, are now very much on the fringe. They are commonly expensive (and hence exclusive) and, in some cases, overtly religious in a way that has only limited appeal. Flagstaff College will be neither religious nor expensive. It will be "affordable" by the standards that now exist (which unfortunately still exclude far too many people), and it will be value-oriented without being wedded to any one religious tradition. Interestingly, Gandhi advocated for private education. So long as a school is dependent on the state for funding, it is not free to follow its own vision of education, nor is it free to be deeply critical of the state. Real academic freedom requires a large measure of economic independence. Schools, he thought, should be as self-sufficient as possible.

At the moment there is very little interest among faculty in transformational change in higher education, and almost no interest among business leaders and politicians. This is hardly surprising in that the colleges and universities we now have support the economic and political order that we have. It is also not surprising that university professors are not, as a rule, advocating for transformational change in higher education. We have all been deeply socialized by our educational past to see the status quo as normative. Transformative change undermines our identity and threatens our expert status. We can be persuaded, perhaps, that change is necessary or inevitable, but we are much more resistant to transformational change. It is possible that the worsening state of the environment and the deteriorating state of our own democracy will make it apparent that something more than educational change is needed. The kind of changes that are now called for are deep-seated changes—radical changes.

Marcus Ford is the author of Beyond the Modern University: Toward a Constructive Postmodern University. *He taught humanities at Northern Arizona University and is now involved in the ulta-small college movement. He has also written on William James and process philosophy.*

References

Arum, R. and J. Roksa. 2011. *Academically Adrift: Limited Learning on College Campuses.* Chicago: University of Chicago Press.

Bateson, G. 1972. *Steps to an Ecology of Mind.* New York: Ballantine Books.

Blumenstyk, G. 2015. *American Higher Education in Crisis? What Everyone Needs to Know.* Chicago: University of Chicago Press.

Bok, D. 2013. *Higher Education in America.* Princeton, NJ: University of Princeton Press.

Bowers, C. 1974. *Cultural Literacy for Freedom.* Eugene, OR: Elan Publishers.

___. 2003. *Mindful Conservatism: Rethinking the Ideological and Educational Basis of an Ecologically Sustainable Future.* Lanham, MD: Rowman & Littlefield.

___. 2011. *Perspectives on the Ideas of Gregory Bateson, Ecological Intelligence, and Educational Reforms.* Eugene, OR: Eco-Justice Press.

___. 2011. *University Reform in an Era of Global Warming.* Eugene, OR: Eco-Justice Press.

___. 2012. *The Way Forward: Educational Reforms that Focus on the Cultural Commons and the Linguistic Roots of the Ecological/Cultural Crisis.* Eugene, OR: Eco-Justice Press.

___. 2013. *In the Grip of the Past: Educational Reforms that Address What Should be Changed and What Should be Conserved.* Eugene, OR: Eco-Justice Press.

___. 2014. *The False Promises of the Digital Revolution: How Computers Transform Education, Work, and International Development in Ways that are Ecologically Unsustainable.* New York: Peter Lang.

___. 2015. *An Ecological and Cultural Critique of the Common Core Curriculum.* New York: Peter Lang.

___. 2016. *Digital Detachment: How Computer Culture Undermines Democracy.* New York: Routledge.

Buber, M. 1937. *I and Thou.* New York: Charles Scribner's Sons.

Carson, R. 1962. *Silent Spring.* New York: Fawcett.Crest.

Clayton, P., and J. Heinzekehr. 2014. *Organic Marxism: An Alternative to Capitalism and Ecological Catastrophe.* Anoka, MN: Process Century.

Clayton, P., and J. Heinzekehr. 2016. *Socialism in Process.* Anoka, MN: Process Century Press.

Club of Rome. 1972. *The Limits to Growth.* New York: Universe Books.

Dawkins, R. 1976. *The Selfish Gene.* New York: Oxford University Press.

Deresiewicz, W. 2014. *Excellent Sheep: The Miseducation of the American Elite & the Way to a Meaningful Life.* New York: Free Press.

Dyson, G. 1998. *Darwin Among the Machines: The Evolution of Global Intelligence.* New York: Basic Books.

Eligon, J, and J. Williams. "On Police Radar for Crimes They Might Commit." *New York Times*, 25 September, 2015.

Foucault, M. 1983. "The Subject and Power," in *Michel Foucault: Beyond Structuralism and Hemeneutics*, by Hubert L. Dreyfus and Paul Rabinow. Chicago: University of Chicago Press.

Frey, C. and G. Osborne. 2013. "The Future of Employment: How Susceptible are Jobs to Computerisation?" <http://www.oxfordmartin.ox.ac.uk/downloads/academic/The_Future_of_Employment.pdf>.

Gray, J. 2015. *The Soul of the Marionette: A Short Inquiry into Human Freedom.* New York: Farrar, Straus and Giroux.

Kolbert, E. 2014. *The Sixth Extinction.* New York: Henry Holt.

Kurzweil, R. 1999. *The Age of Spiritual Machines: When Computers Exceed Human Intelligence.* New York: Viking.

___. 2005. *The Singularity is Near: When Humans Transcend Biology*. New York: Viking Press.

___. 2012. *How to Create a Mind: The Secret of Human Thought Revealed*. New York: Viking Press.

Lakoff, G. and M. Johnson. 1980. *Metaphors We Live By*. Chicago: University of Chicago Press.

___. 1999. *Philosophy in the Flesh: the Embodied Mind & Its Challenge to Western Thought*. New York: Basic Books.

Jucker, R. 2014. *Do We Know What We Are Doing? Reflections on Learning, Knowledge, Economics, Community, and Sustainability*. Newcastle upon Tyne, UK: Cambridge Scholars Publishing.

Leopold, A. 1949. *A Sand County Almanac and Sketches Here and There*. New York: Oxford University Press.

MacIntye, A. 1981. *After Virtue: A Study in Moral Theory*. Notre Dame, IN: University of Notre Dame.

Nietzsche, F. 1937. *The Will to Power*, ed. W. Kaufmann. New York: Charles Scribner's Sons.

Oakshott. M. 1962. *Rationalism in Politics and Other Essays*. London: Methuen.

Ong, W. 1982. *Orality and Literacy: The Technologizing of the Word*. London: Methuen.

Reddy, M. 1979. "The Conduit Metaphor—A Case of Frame Conflict in Our Language about Language." In *Metaphor and Thought*, edited by A. Ortony. Cambridge, GB: Cambridge University Press, 284–323.

Spring, J. 2015. *A Perfect Life*. Phoenix Books. <http:/amazon.com/Perfect-Life-Joel>.

Stock, G. 1993. *Metaman: The Merging of Humans and Machines in a Global Superorganism*. New York. Doubleday.

Thich Nhat Hanh. 2002. *No Death, No Fear*. New York: Riverhead Books.

Wilson, E. 1998. *Consilience: The Unity of Knowledge*. New York: Alfred A. Knopf.

Wittes, B. and G. Blum. 2015. *The Future of Violence: Robots and Germs, Hackers and Drones—Confronting a New Age of Threat*. New York: Basic Books.